Date: _____

Draw line graphs

1 **a)** Use the information in the table to complete

Feet	0	2	3	4
Inches	0	24	36	48

b) Now use the graph to fill in the missing information.

1 foot = ☐ inches

10 feet = ☐ inches

$3\frac{1}{2}$ feet = ☐ inches

$5\frac{1}{4}$ feet = ☐ inches

30 inches = ☐ feet

100 inches = ☐ feet

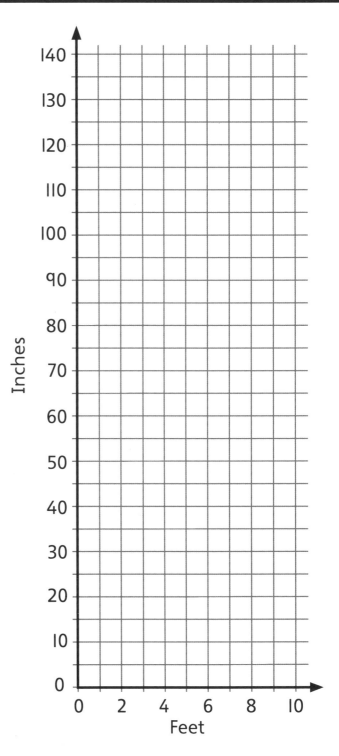

2 This table shows the number of people living in a village over time.

Year	1980	1990	2000	2010	2020	2030
Population	800	1,100	1,500	2,300	3,400	

Use this information to draw a line graph of the population and predict the population in 2030.

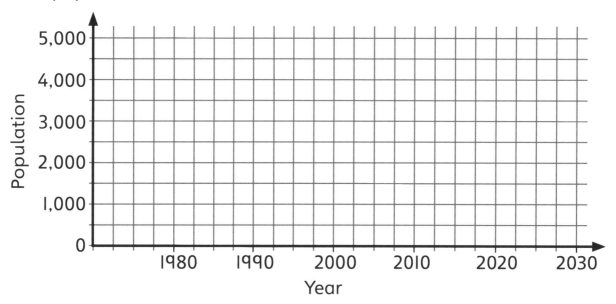

3 This table shows the flight of a firework. Complete the line graph from the information and predict when the firework will land.

Time in seconds	0	2	4	6	8	10	
Height in metres	0	20	30	35	28	15	0

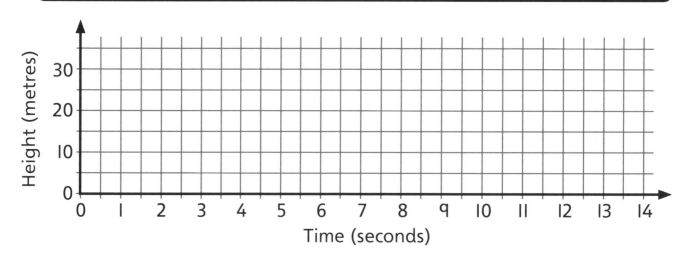

5 A market stall sells dog food, cat food and bird seed. This pie chart shows the sales for one weekend.

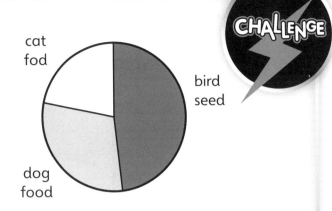

cat fod

bird seed

dog food

CHALLENGE

a) Estimate the fraction of the total sales for each type of food.

Show that your fraction estimates add up to 1.

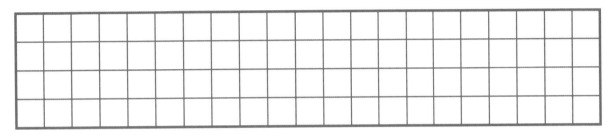

b) If the total sales were £300, work out the value of the sales for each type of food.

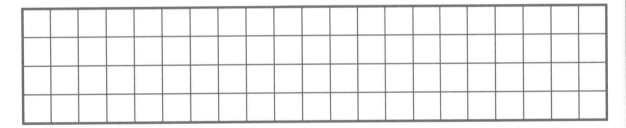

Reflect

What fractions can you see in this pie chart?

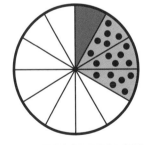

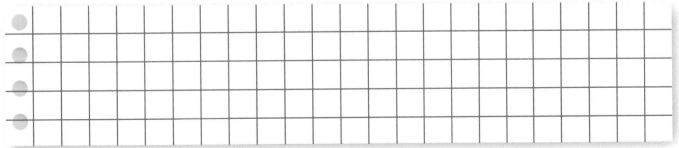

Date: _____

Pie charts and fractions ②

1 A class looked for different species of tree. Complete the table using the information in the pie chart.

Type of tree	Number seen
birch	
oak	12
pine	
fir	
Total	

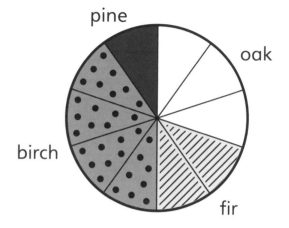

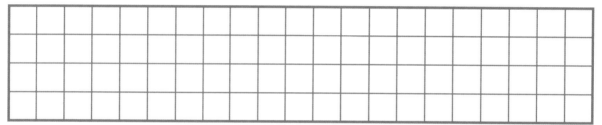

2 There were 24 sightings of sparrows.

a) How many birds were seen altogether?

b) How many blackbirds were seen?

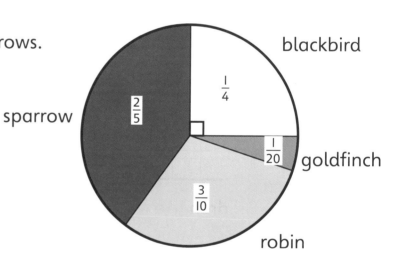

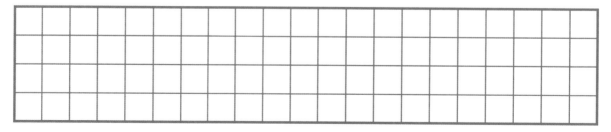

3 Olivia and Luis threw bean bags at a target. Olivia hit the outer target 28 times. This was 2 fewer times than Luis.

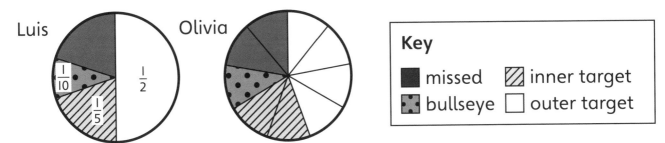

Luis   Olivia

Key

■ missed   ▨ inner target
⊡ bullseye   ☐ outer target

Did Luis throw more bean bags than Olivia?

4 This pie chart shows which school dinners the children in Class 6 prefer.

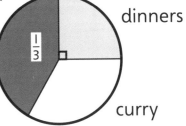

roast dinners

pizza $\frac{1}{3}$

curry

a) What fraction like curry?

b) 96 children like roast dinners. How many children like pizza and curry?

5 This pie chart shows the proportion of ingredients in a tropical fruit drink.

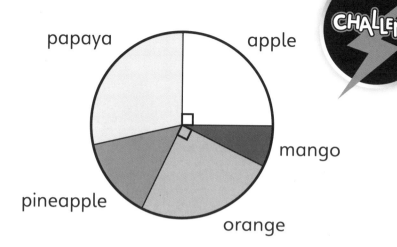

There is twice as much pineapple as mango.

There is twice as much papaya as pineapple.

a) What fraction is mango?

b) In 350 ml of fruit drink, how much more papaya is needed than pineapple?

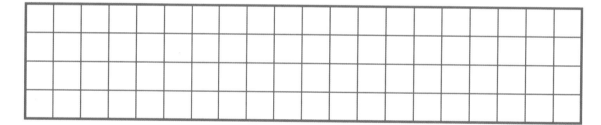

Reflect

Write a problem for a partner that gives them a fraction of a pie chart, and asks them to work out the whole. Sketch a pie chart to go with the problem.

Date: 3.7.23

Pie charts and percentages

1   Complete the missing percentages.

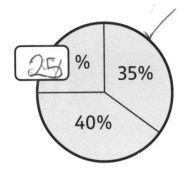 25%   35%   40%

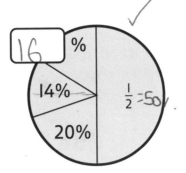 16%   14%   20% $\frac{1}{2}$ = 50

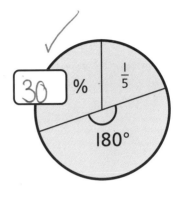 30% $\frac{1}{5}$ 180°

2   60 people voted for a sports captain.

How many votes did each person receive?

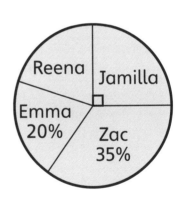

Jamilla = 15 votes ✓   1 5
Emma = 10 votes ° 12   1 0
Zac = 25 votes ° 12   1 0
Reena = 20 votes ° 21   2 5
   6 0

27

3 This pie chart shows the results of a survey about shopping for clothes.

56 people said they go to shopping centres. How many more people shop online than use second-hand shops?

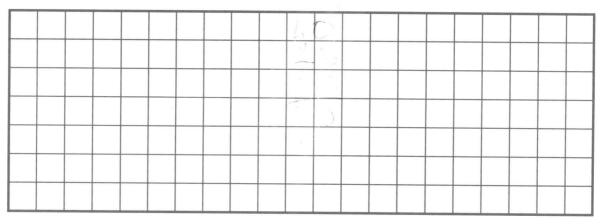

4 In one football season, the Rovers scored 48 penalties and missed 32. The pie chart shows what United scored.

Which team was more successful at penalties? Justify your answer.

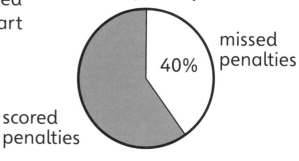

United penalty kicks

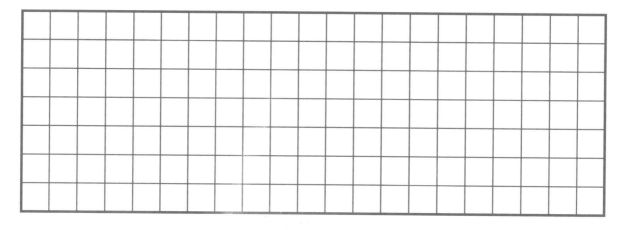

5 These pie charts show the types of tree in Hetiddy Woods and Lanhay Forest.

CHALLENGE

Hetiddy Woods
80 trees

willow
birch
36°
54°
oak
180°
pine

Lanhay Forest
200 trees

willow
oak
$\frac{1}{5}$
30%
birch
pine

How many more birch trees are there in Lanhay Forest than in Hetiddy Woods?

Reflect

Draw a pie chart that shows $\frac{1}{4}$, 10% and 15%. Show the remaining percentage and explain how you calculated this.

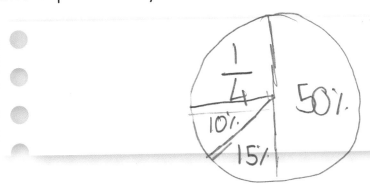

Date: _____

Introduction to the mean

1 **a)** Draw three new towers that show the mean height of these three towers.

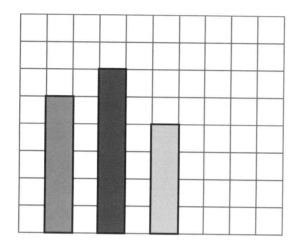 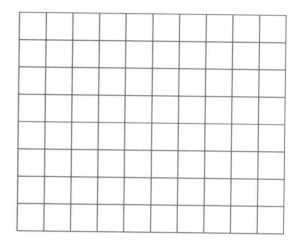

b) Draw four new rows of counters that show the mean number of counters.

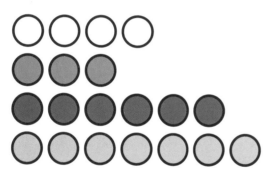 

2 What is the mean number of marbles in the bags?

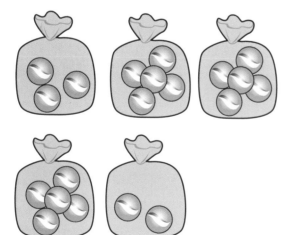 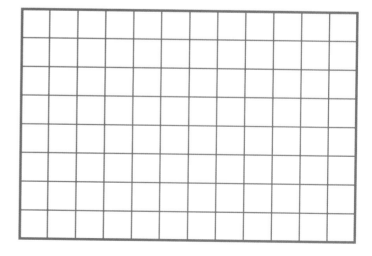

3 Match groups of dice that show the same mean number of dots.

A

C

B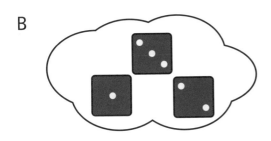

D

4 Circle the group with the greatest mean.

A (4 1 1 2)

B 2 0 0 2

C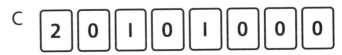

D

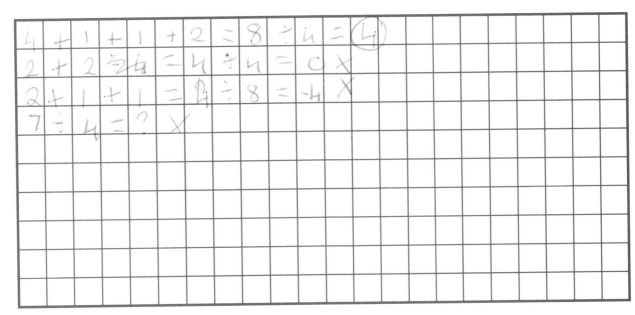

5 Find the mean of the two numbers shown on each number line and mark the mean on the number line.

CHALLENGE

a)

|————————————————————————————————|
100   200

b)

|————————————————————————————————|
2,000   4,000

c)

|————————————————————————————————|
198   202

d)

|————————————————————————————————|
0   7

Explain what you notice.

_____

_____

_____

Reflect

Describe two ways to find the mean of these numbers: 4, 5 and 6.

_____

_____

_____

Date: _____

Calculate the mean

→ Textbook 6C p44

1 Complete the bar models to show the mean number of dots on each group of dice.

a)

2	4	6	4

2 + 4 + 6 + 4 = ☐

☐ ÷ 4 = ☐

b)

1	5	6	2

c)

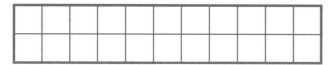

2 Find the mean capacity of these paint pots.

500 ml   1·5 l   2 l   1 l

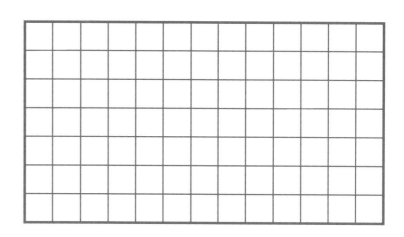

33

3 These tables show how much money two families spend on food each week.

Which family has the greater mean weekly spend?

Clark Family		
Week 1	Week 2	Week 3
£74	£85	£69

Kapoor Family			
Week 1	Week 2	Week 3	Week 4
£72	£70	£81	£78

4 Find the mean length of all the planks of wood.

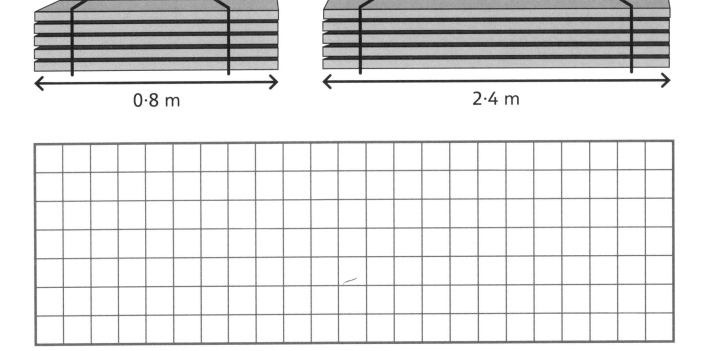

0·8 m   2·4 m

5 Here are the scores from a gymnastics competition.
   The winner is the person with the greatest mean score.
   Who came first, second and third?

CHALLENGE

Alex	5	5·5	5	5·5	–
Richard	5	5	6	6	5
Lexi	4	8	10	–	–
Bella	0	10	10	10	2

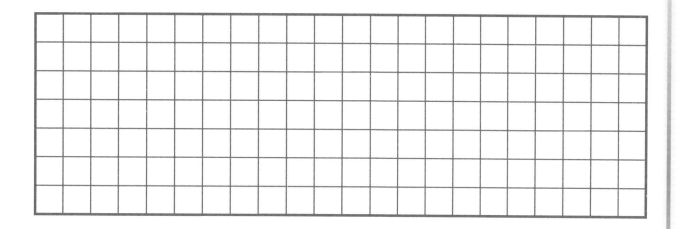

First: _____ Second: _____ Third: _____

Reflect

Complete this sentence.

To find the mean of a set of numbers, you _____

_____

_____

35

Date: _____

Problem solving – mean

1 Draw another tower in each group, so that the mean height of both groups is 5.

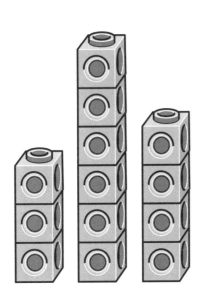 

2 The mean number of pets the children in the table have is 4.

How many pets does Emma have?

Bella	2 pets
Andy	12 pets
Danny	1 pet
Emma	

4	4	4	4

3 4 stalls earn money at a cake sale. The mean amount of money earned is £1·50. How much did the fourth group earn?

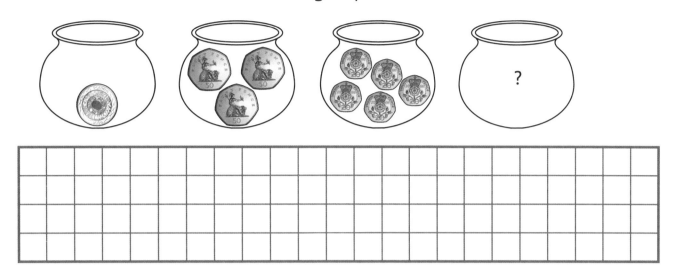

4 The mean of these sets of number cards is 3. What could the missing numbers be?

a)

| 2 | 3 | 3 | |

b)

| 2 | 3 | 3 | | |

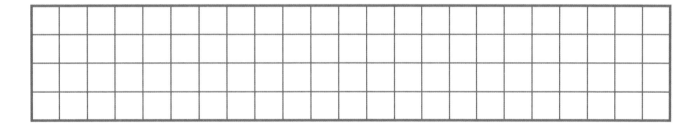

5 Draw the water levels in jugs B and E so that the mean volume of all of the jugs is $\frac{1}{4}$ litre.

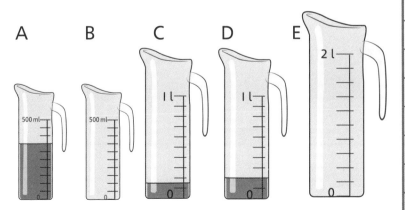

6 Find a solution to each set of clues.

CHALLENGE

a) Two even numbers with a mean of 5.

b) Three odd numbers with a mean of 5.

c) A set of 4 numbers. The difference between the greatest and the smallest is 10. The mean is 4.

d) A set of numbers that are not whole, but the mean is a whole number.

Reflect

Draw two different sets of number cards which each have a mean of 7·5. Explain your choice of numbers to a partner.

Date: _____

End of unit check

My journal

↓ Textbook 6C p52

1 Use the information below to draw a line graph to convert $ (dollars) and £ (pounds). Find the approximate number of £s that equal $19.

Use these numbers: 15 dollars is worth 10 pounds.

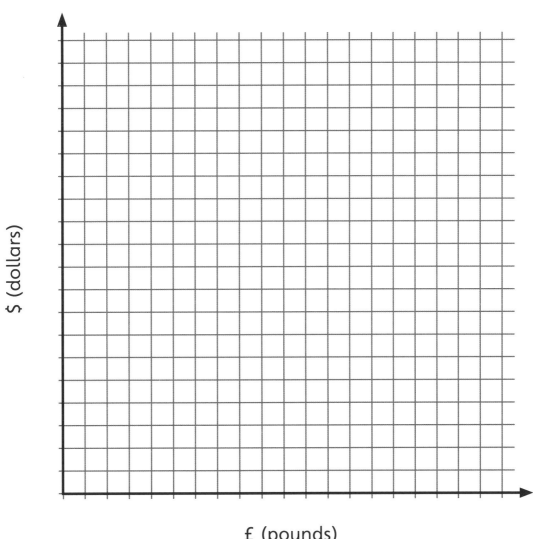

£ (pounds)

2 Add notes to this diagram to show when you would use each type of chart and why its features would be useful.

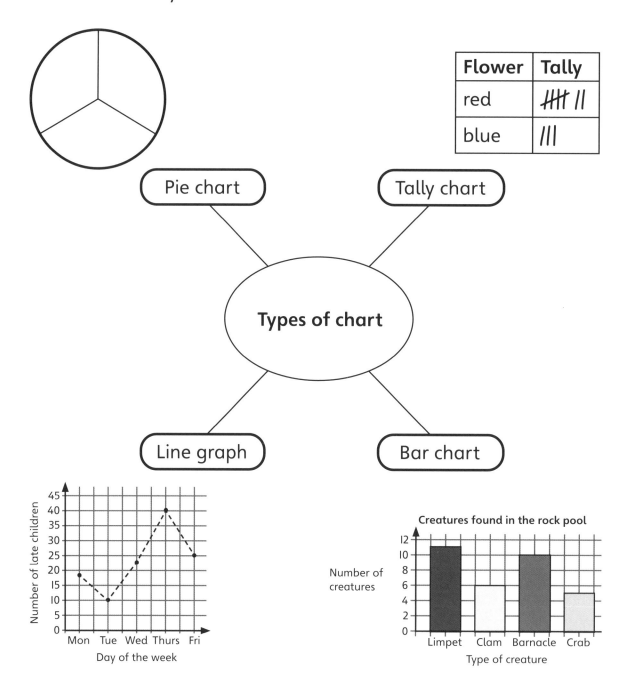

Flower	Tally
red	Ж||
blue	|||

Power check

How do you feel about your work in this unit?

Power play

You will need:

- A grid with the *y*-axis going from ⁻50 to 50 and the *x*-axis going from 0 to 20.

How to play:

Play this game with a partner. Choose who is Player 1 and who is Player 2.

Take it in turns to roll two dice. Add the scores on both dice. If the result is an even number, add it to the current score. If the result is an odd number, subtract it from the current score. Each player has 10 turns.

Start at 0. Mark the new score at the turn number on the *x*-axis. Join the points each time you plot a new score to draw a line graph.

Player 1 wins if the line ends on a positive score. Player 2 wins if the line ends on a negative score.

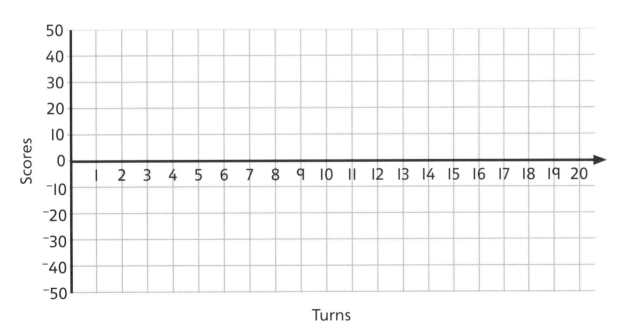

Draw your own axes and play a few times, but choose different rules. You could multiply the dice or find the difference.

Date:_____

Measure and classify angles

1 Write down the size of each angle.

a)

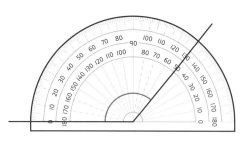

i30 ~~80~~ °

c)

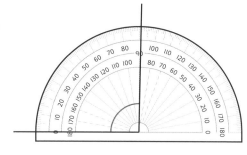

90 °

b)

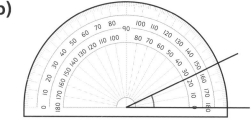

25 °

d)

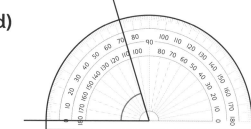

73 °

2 Draw lines to match each angle with the correct measurement.

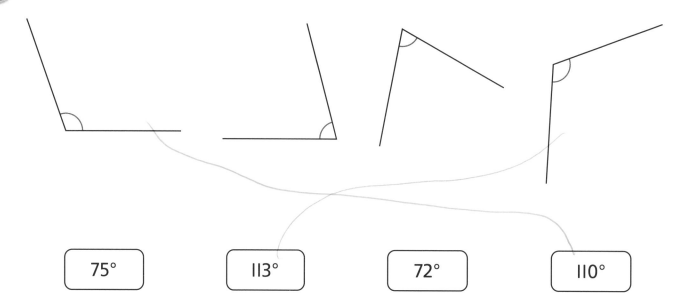

75°   113°   72°   110°

42

3 **a)** Measure and label all of the interior angles.

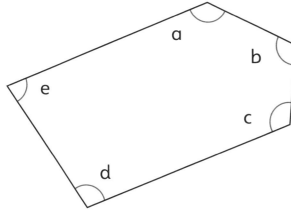 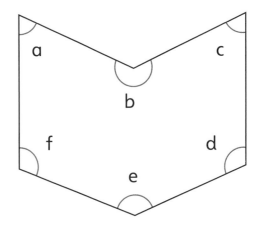

a = _____°   d = _____°   a = _____°   d = _____°

b = _____°   e = _____°   b = _____°   e = _____°

c = _____°   c = _____°   f = _____°

b) Which one of the following is a regular shape? Explain your answer.

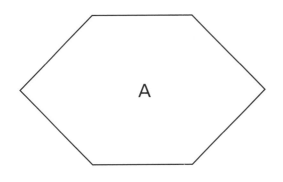 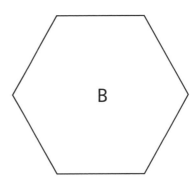

A   B

_____

_____

4 Mo says, 'These angles increase in size.' Is he correct? Discuss your answer with a partner.

 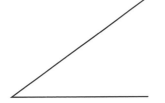 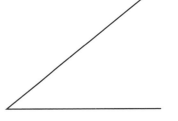

5 Complete each symmetrical figure. Measure and label all the interior angles.

CHALLENGE

a)

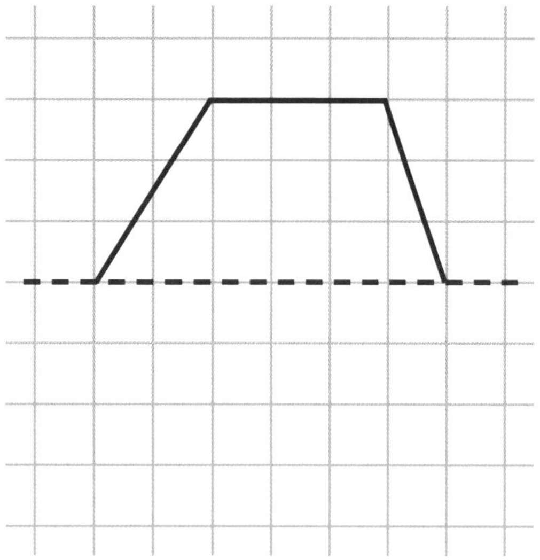

b)

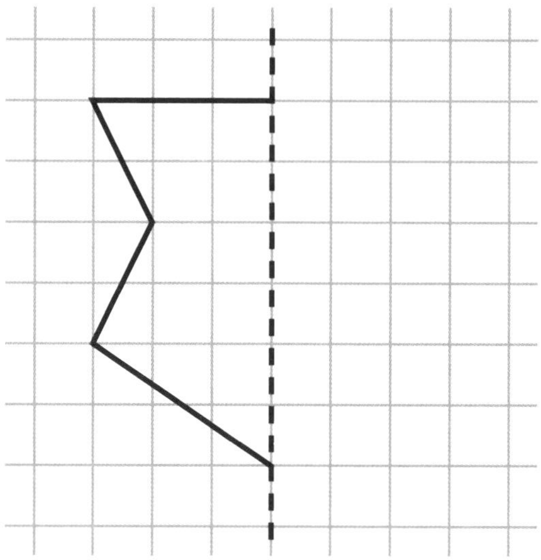

Explain what you notice.

_____

_____

Reflect

What simple mistakes might be made when measuring angles?
Write a checklist for avoiding these mistakes.

- _____
- _____
- _____

Vertically opposite angles

1 Complete each missing angle.

a)

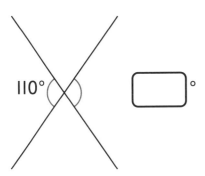 110° ☐°

c)

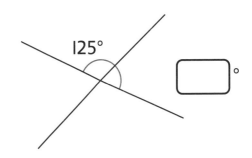 125° ☐°

b)

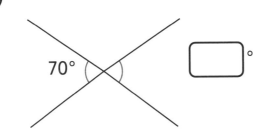 70° ☐°

d)

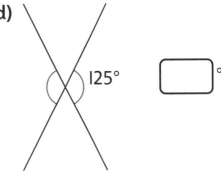 125° ☐°

2 Circle the diagram that does **not** show vertically opposite angles.

 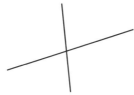 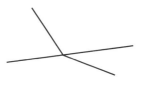 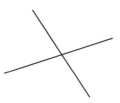

3 Calculate each of the missing angles below.

a)

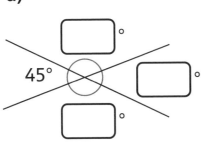 45°

b)

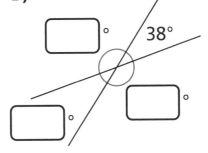 38°

c)

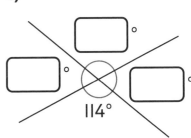 114°

45

4 Draw a line so that there are two 135° angles.

5 Complete the table below.

Experiment 1   Experiment 2   Experiment 3

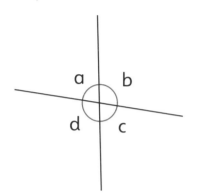 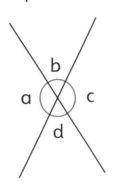 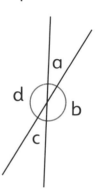

In Experiment 1, angle a is 20° less than angle b.

In Experiment 2, angle a is twice as large as angle b.

In Experiment 3, angle a is one-fifth the size of angle d.

	Angle a	Angle b	Angle c	Angle d
Experiment 1				
Experiment 2				
Experiment 3				

6 Calculate the missing angles.

CHALLENGE

a)

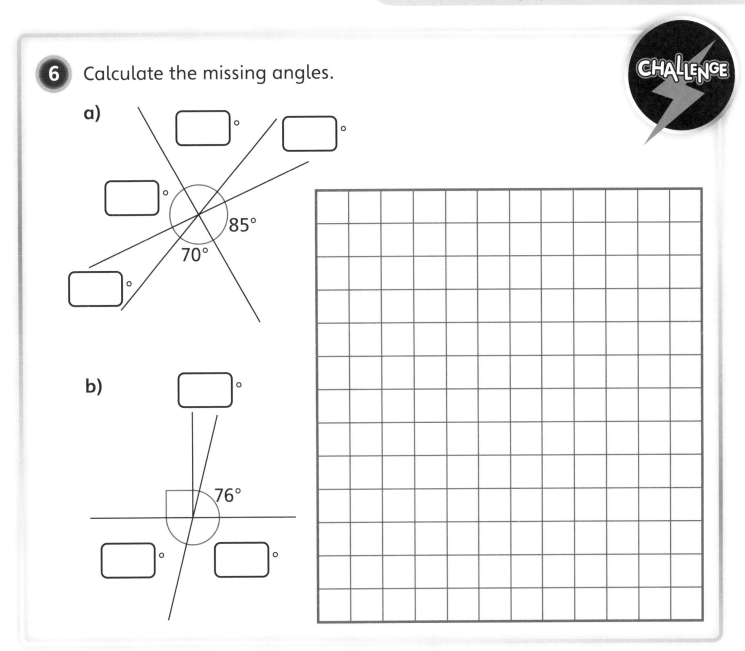

85°

70°

b)

76°

Reflect

Explain why vertically opposite angles must be equal.

Date:_____

Angles in a triangle

1 **a)** Circle all the angles that have been measured incorrectly.

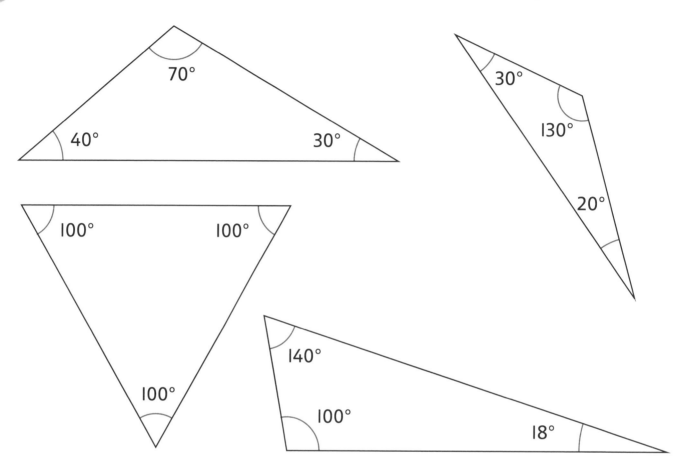

b) Draw this triangle accurately and then measure the missing angle.

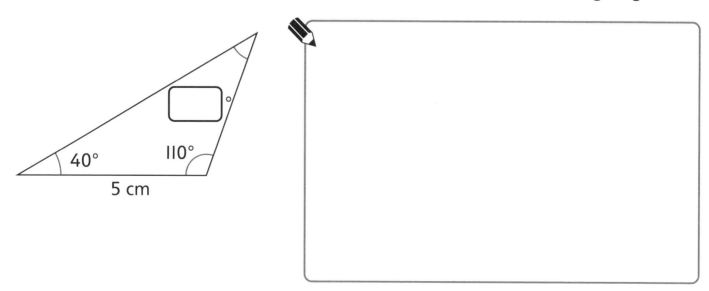

2 The corners from these paper triangles have been torn off. Draw lines to match the angles to the triangles they are from.

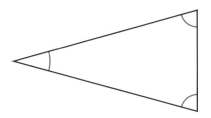

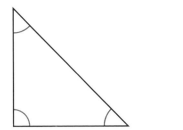

3 Tick to show which statements are always true, sometimes true and never true. Discuss your answers with a partner.

A triangle has …	Always true	Sometimes true	Never true
… three acute angles.			
… two right angles.			
… a right angle and an obtuse angle.			
… three different angles.			
… angles that add up to 180°.			
… at least two acute angles.			

4 In each circle, join three dots to form a different triangle. Measure and write the measurements of all of the angles in the triangles and check that they add up to 180° in each triangle.

CHALLENGE

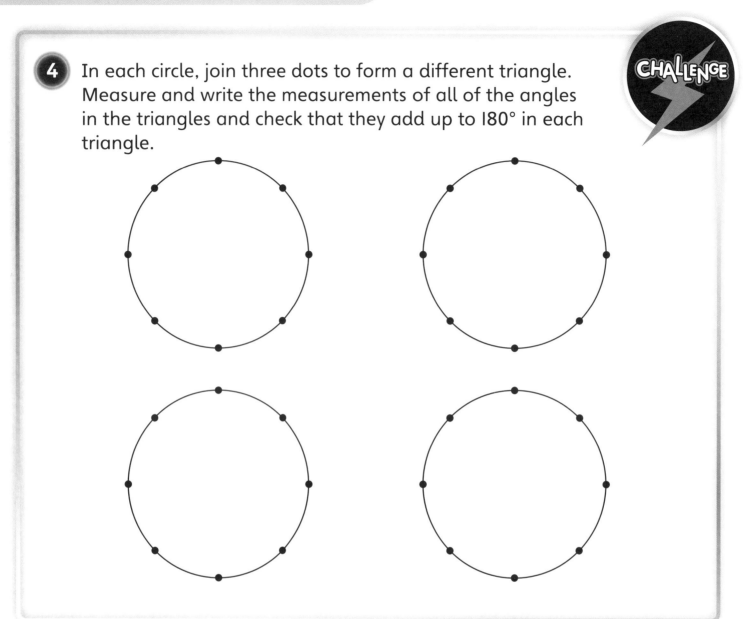

Reflect

What is the sum of the angles in a triangle? How do you know? How can you prove it?

_____

_____

_____

Angles in a triangle – missing angles

1 Calculate the missing angles.

a)

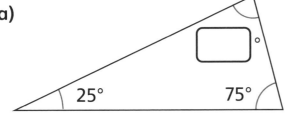

c)

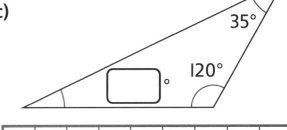

→ Textbook 6C p68

b)

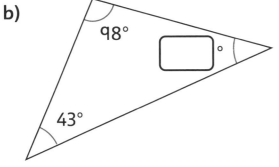

d)

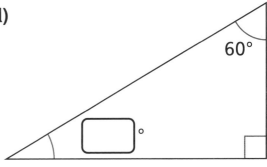

2 Measure two angles and then calculate the third, showing your calculation.

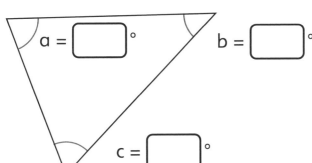

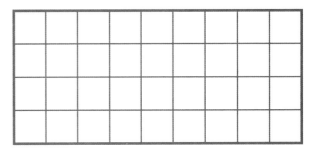

3 Draw lines to make groups of three angles that could form a triangle.

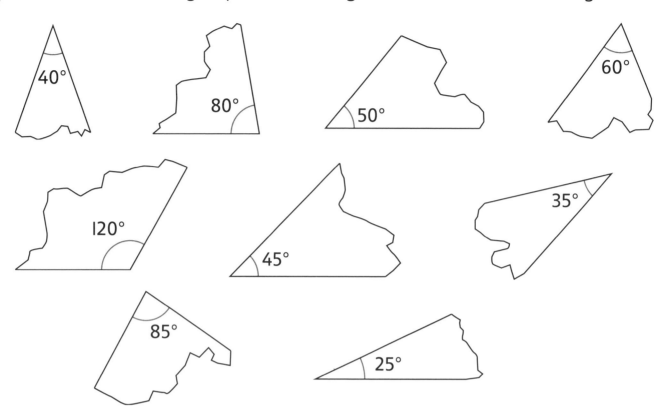

4 Calculate the missing angles.

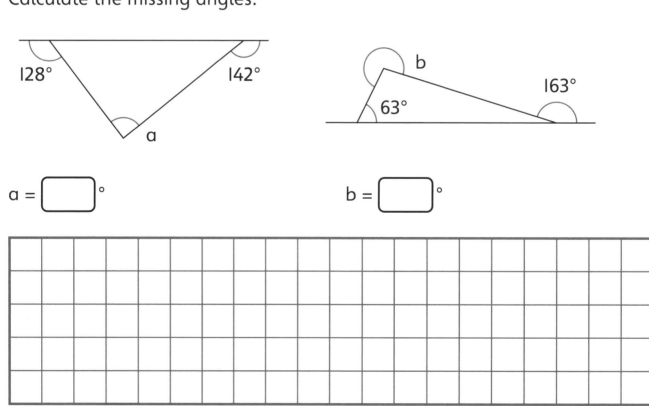

a = [   ]°

b = [   ]°

5 This triangle has been drawn in a rectangle. Calculate the missing angles.

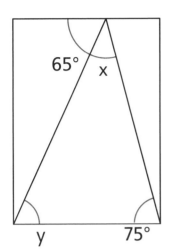

x = [ ]°   y = [ ]°

Reflect

Draw two different diagrams for triangles with a missing angle of 50 degrees. How did you work out the angles for the triangles?

Date:_____

Angles in a triangle – special cases

1 Mark the equal lengths on these triangles, using the correct notation. Look at the angles to help you.

a) 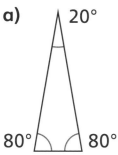 20° 80° 80°

b) 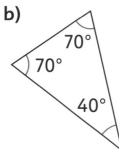 70° 70° 40°

c) 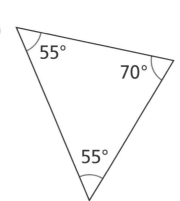 55° 70° 55°

d) 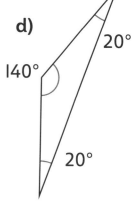 20° 140° 20°

2 Calculate the missing angles in each triangle below.

a) 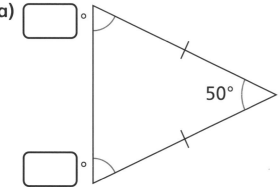 50°

c)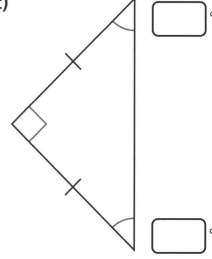

b) 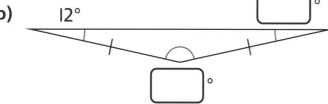 12°

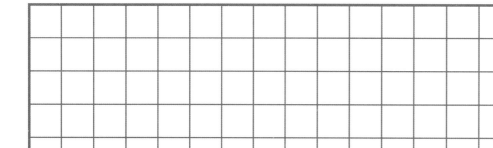

3 Tick the isosceles triangle and mark both its equal lengths and its equal angles.

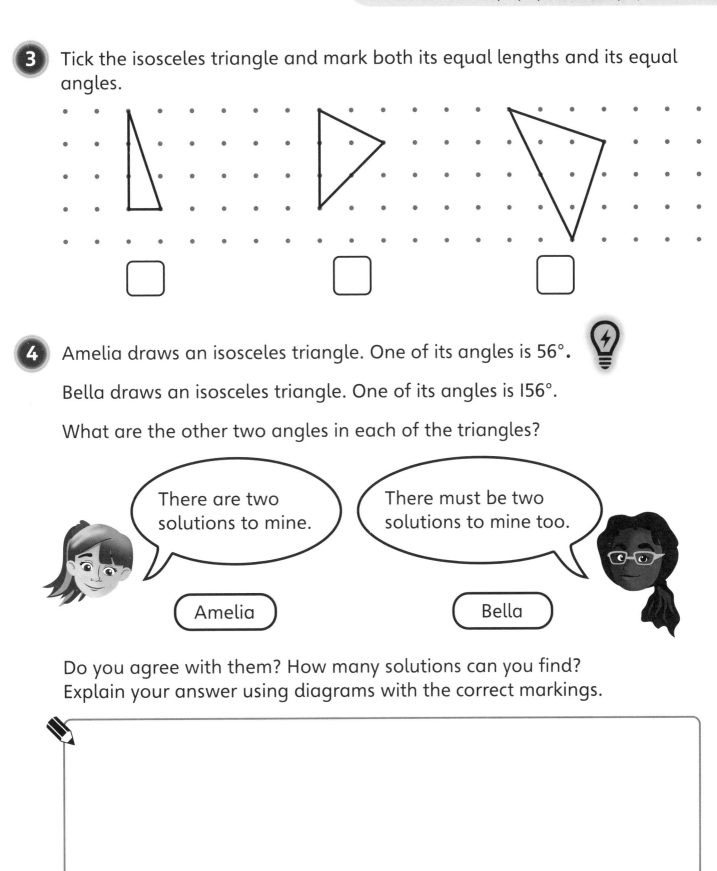

4 Amelia draws an isosceles triangle. One of its angles is 56°.

Bella draws an isosceles triangle. One of its angles is 156°.

What are the other two angles in each of the triangles?

There are two solutions to mine.

Amelia

There must be two solutions to mine too.

Bella

Do you agree with them? How many solutions can you find?
Explain your answer using diagrams with the correct markings.

5 Calculate the missing angles.

CHALLENGE

a)

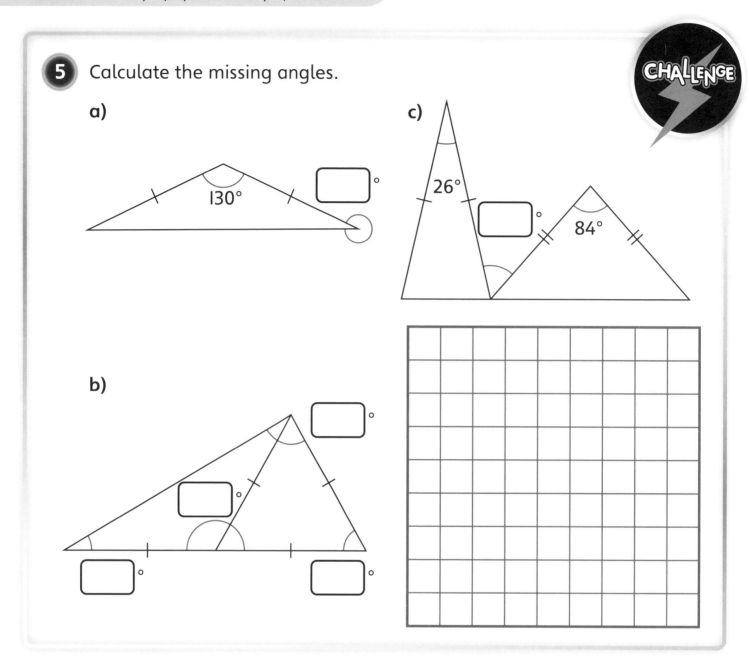

b)

Reflect

Create a missing angle problem involving isosceles triangles.

Angles in quadrilaterals

1 Join each shape to the correct label.

a) 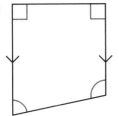 b) 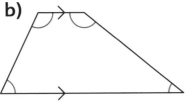 c) 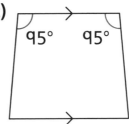 d)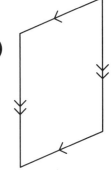

| Parallelogram | Isosceles trapezium | Scalene trapezium | Right-angled trapezium |

2 The following shapes have been made inside rectangles. Calculate the missing angles.

a)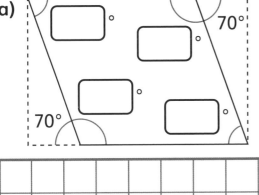

b)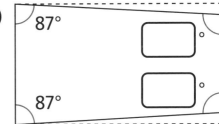

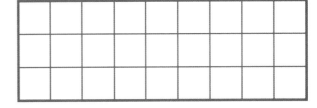

3 Add markings to show any parallel lines or equal lengths in the shapes below.

a) 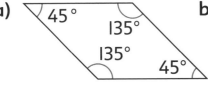 b) 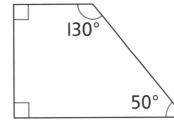 c)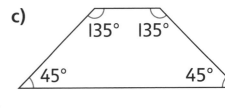

4 Calculate the missing angles.

a)

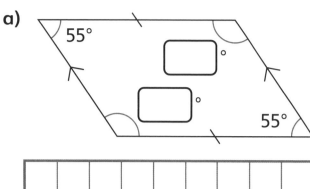

b)

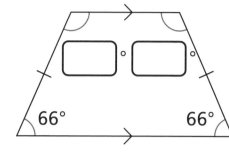

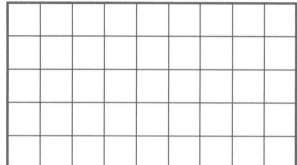

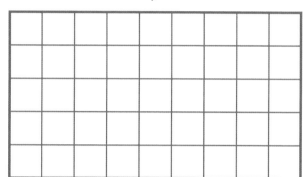

5 Decide if each statement is always true, sometimes true or never true. Explain your reasoning and use diagrams to support your thinking.

A parallelogram has three acute angles.

_____

_____

_____

_____

_____

A trapezium has four different angles.

_____

_____

_____

_____

_____

6 **a)** How many different parallelograms can you create on these grids?

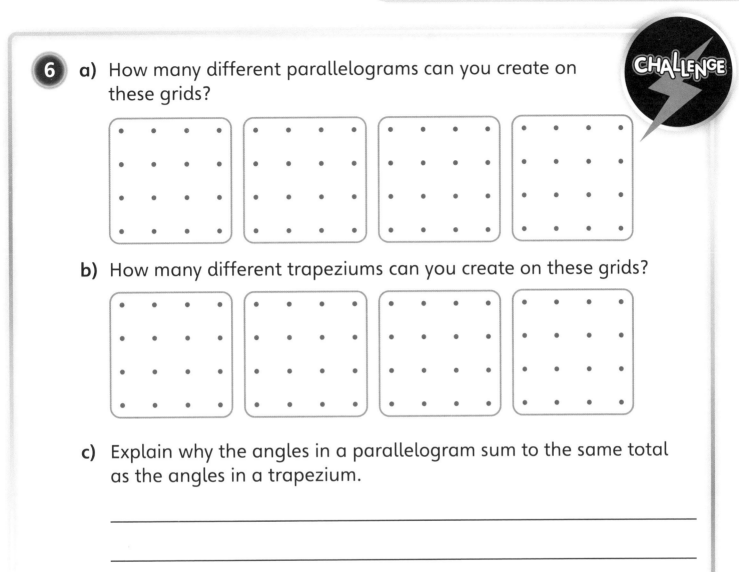

b) How many different trapeziums can you create on these grids?

c) Explain why the angles in a parallelogram sum to the same total as the angles in a trapezium.

_____

_____

_____

Reflect

Draw a diagram to explain what you know about the angle sums in trapeziums and parallelograms.

Date:_____

Angles in polygons

1 Calculate the missing angle in each shape.

a)
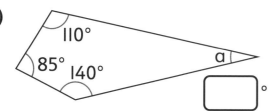

c)
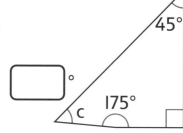

b)
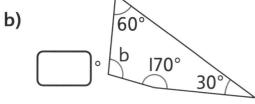

d)
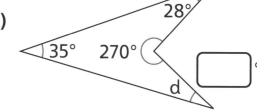

2 In each shape, one angle has been measured incorrectly. Identify this angle and calculate its correct value.

a)
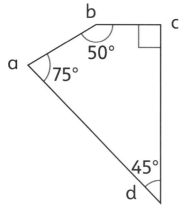

b)
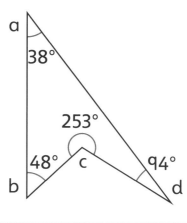

Textbook 6C p80

3 Draw lines to split each shape into triangles. Write the total sum of the angles for each shape.

a)

total = ☐°

b)

total = ☐°

c)

total = ☐°

4 Emma says, 'I split this shape into 4 triangles. There are 180° in each triangle and 180 × 4 = 720°, so this quadrilateral must have internal angles that add up to 720°.'

Can you explain Emma's mistake?

_____

_____

5 Calculate the interior angles of a regular decagon.

each interior angle = ☐° total of all interior angles = ☐°

61

6 **a)** This regular hexagon has been drawn inside a rectangle.

Calculate angles a and b.

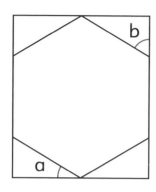

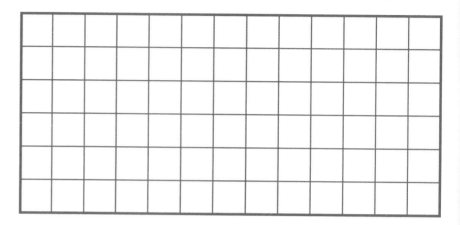

b) How many angles can you calculate in this diagram of a pentagon drawn inside a rectangle? Write the angle measurements on the shape.

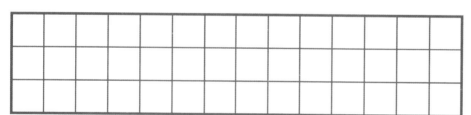

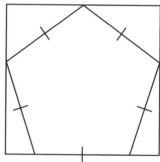

Reflect

Create a missing angle problem involving a quadrilateral. The missing angle should be 40°.

Circles

1 **a)** Draw 20 dots, each one exactly 25 mm from the cross.

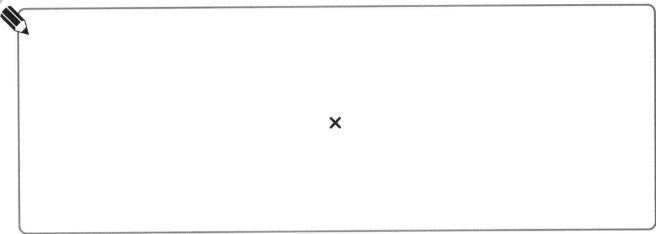

×

b) Complete the sentence.
The dots are on a circle with a radius of [ ] mm.

2 Label whether each diagram shows the radius or the diameter. Measure and write the radius and diameter for each circle.

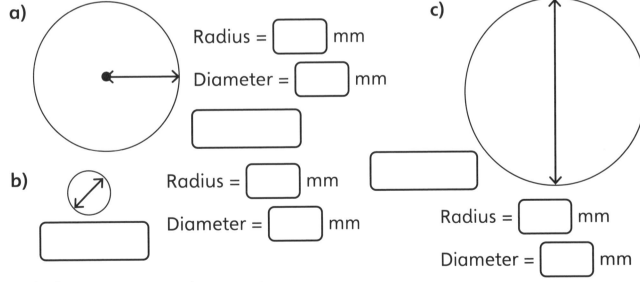

a)

Radius = [ ] mm

Diameter = [ ] mm

[   ]

b)

[   ]

Radius = [ ] mm

Diameter = [ ] mm

c)

[   ]

Radius = [ ] mm

Diameter = [ ] mm

3 Tick the statements that are true.

The radius is twice as long as the diameter. [ ]

The diameter passes through the centre of the circle. [ ]

If the radius is x, then the diameter is $x + x$. [ ]

63

Textbook 6C p84

4 Calculate the radius of each circle.

a)

8 mm

b)

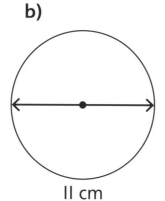

11 cm

c)

6·8 cm

d)

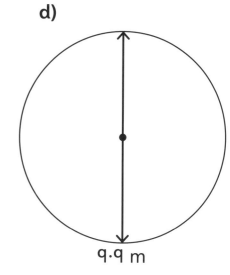

9·9 m

Radius =

☐ mm

Radius =

☐ cm

Radius =

☐ cm

Radius =

☐ m

5 a) Calculate the radius of a 2p coin.

Coins not actual size

13 cm

Radius = ☐ mm

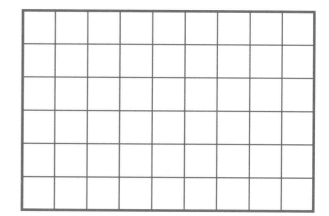

b) This is a 5p coin.

Calculate the length of the line.

18 mm

The line is ☐ mm

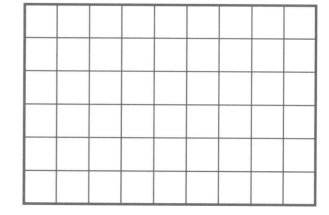

6 **a)** The perimeter of the triangle is 16·8 cm.
   What is the radius of one of the circles?

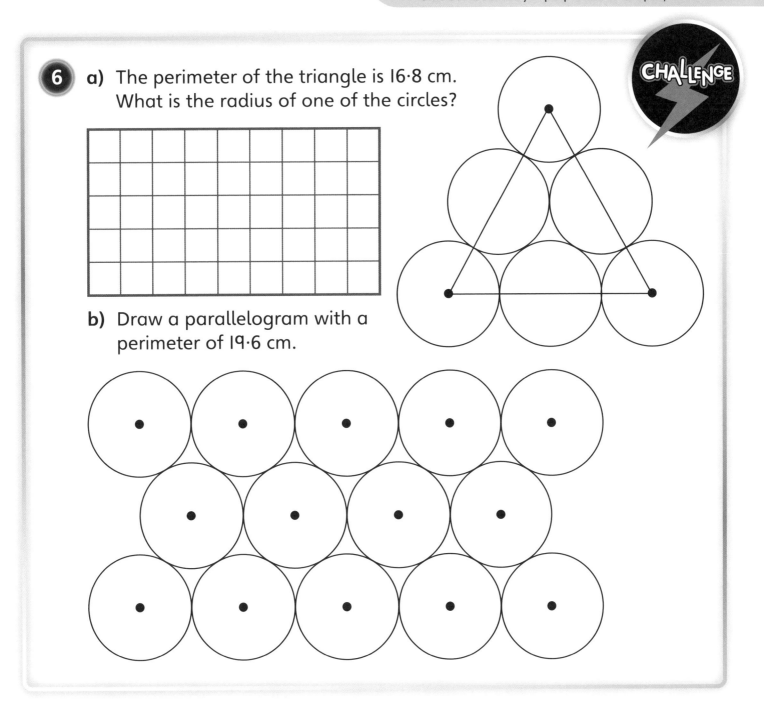

b) Draw a parallelogram with a
   perimeter of 19·6 cm.

Reflect

Describe how to draw a circle with a diameter of 4 cm.

_____

_____

Date:_____

Parts of a circle

1 Tick the diagram that has been labelled correctly.

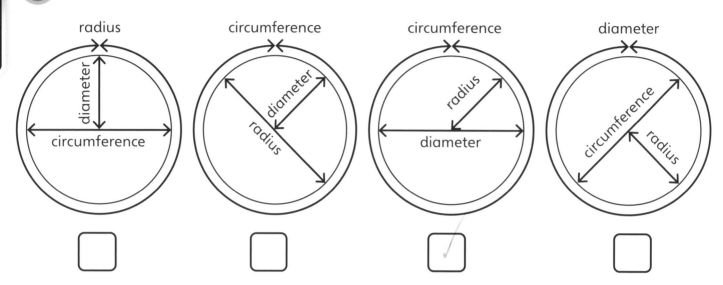

2 **a)** On each circle, draw two dots on the circumference. Then join these dots to the centre to form triangles. Measure one angle in each triangle and then calculate the other angles.

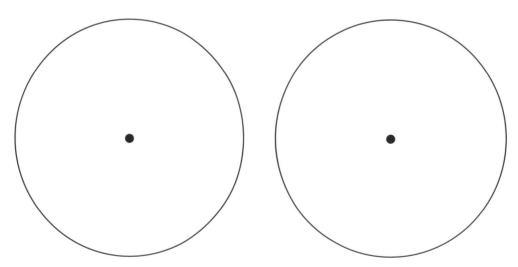

b) What types of triangle are formed? Explain why.

_____

_____

_____

3 Join dots to form these quadrilaterals: a parallelogram, an isosceles trapezium, a rhombus and a kite.

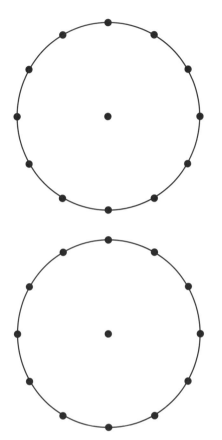
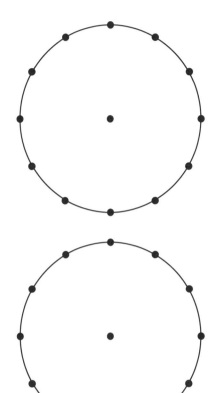

4 Form a triangle using the diameter and a point on the circumference. Work out the angles of the triangle. You should only need to measure one of the angles.

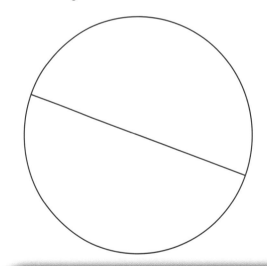

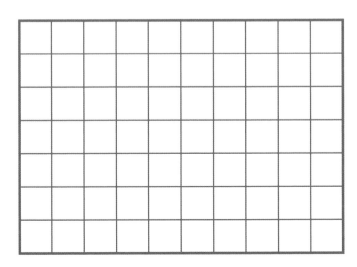

You do not need to measure the right angle.

5 Find the approximate area of this circle.

I will count the whole squares and then the half squares.

Reflect

Describe how to use a circle to draw an isosceles triangle.

Draw shapes accurately

1 Draw these three angles. In each case, the first line has been drawn for you.

a) 60° **b)** 70° **c)** 80°

Textbook 6C p92

_____   _____   _____

2 Use the space below to draw this shape accurately.

Find and label the missing measurements to the nearest degree and cm.

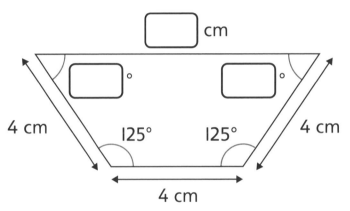

69

3 Complete the three parallelograms, ensuring the angles and lengths are correct.

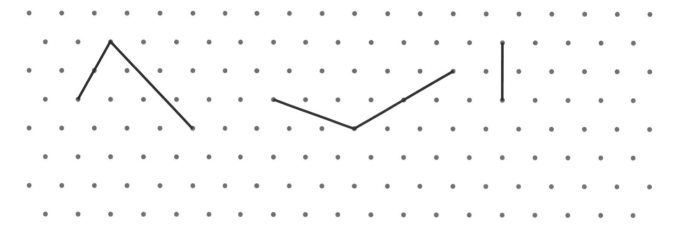

4 Two lines of three different kites have been drawn. Complete the kites.

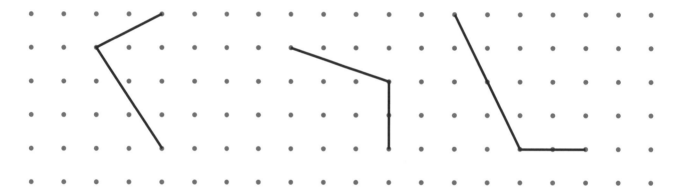

5 Draw a kite, a rhombus and a rectangle. Make sure they are accurate.

6 One side of each of two rectangles has been drawn.

Each rectangle has an area of 12 cm². Complete the rectangles by drawing the sides and angles accurately.

CHALLENGE

a)

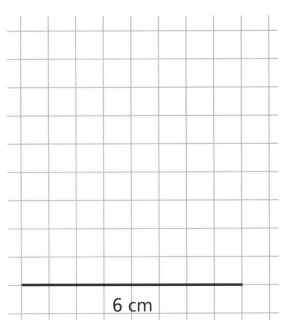

6 cm

b)

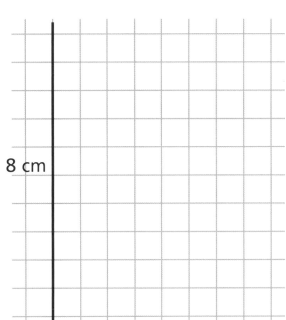

8 cm

Reflect

Lee is drawing a 100° angle. What are the steps he needs to take? What mistakes does he need to avoid?

Date:_____

Nets of 3D shapes ❶

1 Draw lines to match the nets to the 3D shapes.

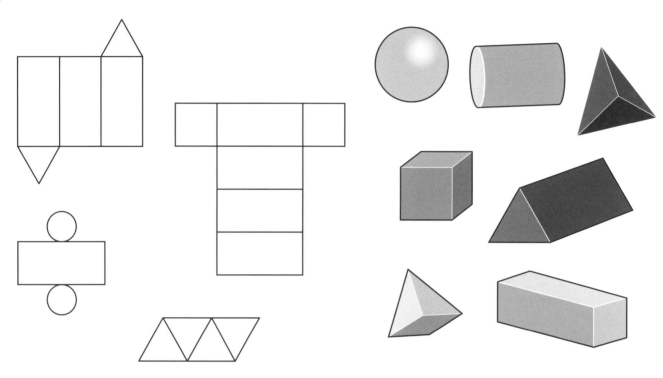

2 Tick any nets that will fold correctly to form a pyramid.

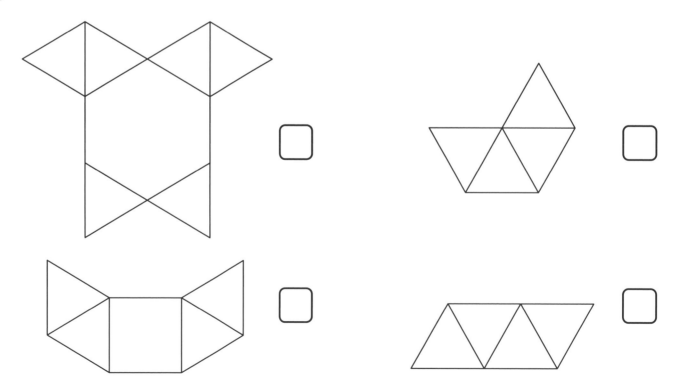

3 This net forms a hexagonal prism. The shapes on the faces should be in pairs on opposite faces. Draw one more circle, one more triangle and one more square, so that there are pairs of shapes on opposite faces of the prism.

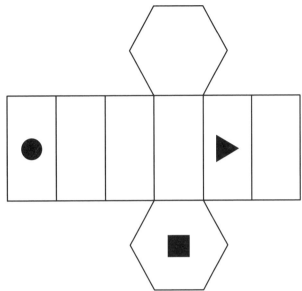

4 The top half of this cuboid is painted and the bottom half is white. Complete the shading on the net.

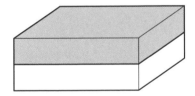

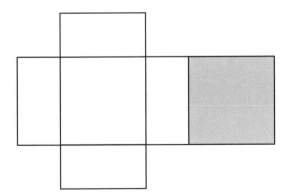

73

5 Complete the net of this cuboid.

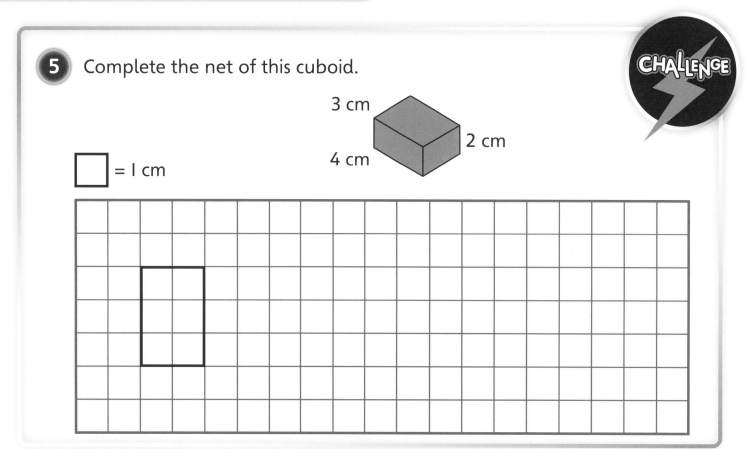

□ = 1 cm

Reflect

Draw a net for a pyramid.

Nets of 3D shapes ❷

1   Tick the nets that will form a cube.

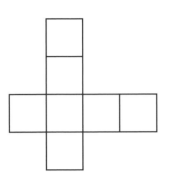   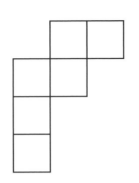   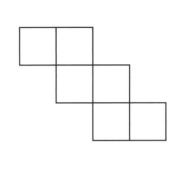

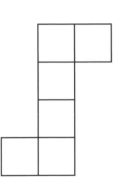   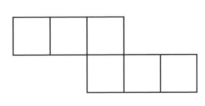   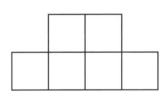

2   Complete the net of a cube in three different ways, using the diagrams below.

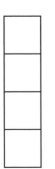   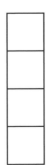   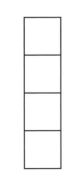

75

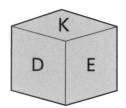

 On this cube, three faces have an animal on them. Each animal's name begins with the letter on the opposite face.

Draw three possible nets for this cube.

 Complete the shading on the net for this cube.

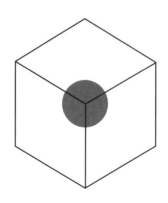

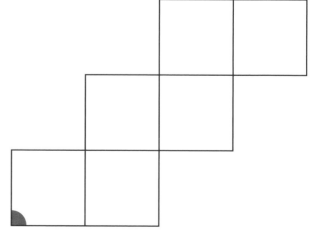

5 Here is a net of a cube. What is the volume of the cube?

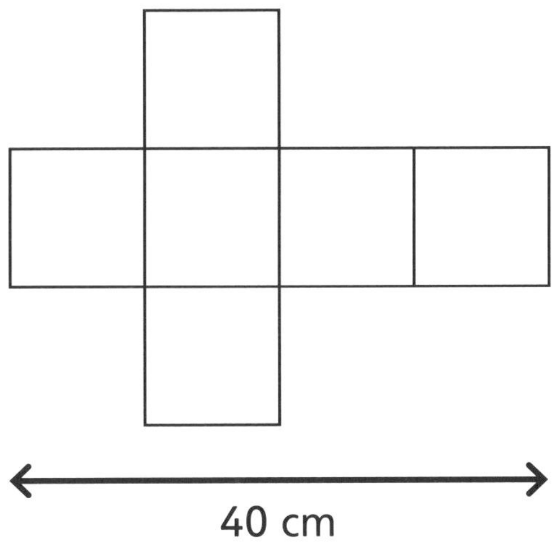

CHALLENGE

40 cm

Reflect

Provide some advice for how to spot if a net will form a cube.

Date: _____

End of unit check

My journal

1) Calculate the size of the angles p, q and r.

Angle q is twice as big as angle r.

Angle r is three times as big as angle p.

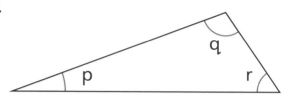

180°

p	

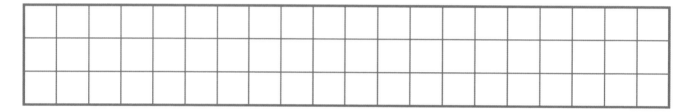

2) Two straight lines cross a square.

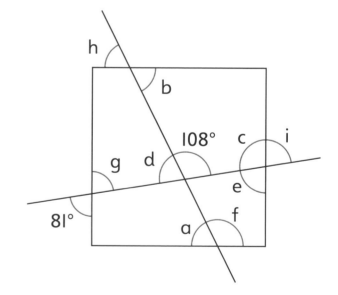

Which angles can you work out?

Explain how you worked them out.

_____

_____

_____

3 Write the correct label under each net.

Cube   Prism   Pyramid   Not a net

A

C

E

G

cube   _pyramid_   _Prism_   _Not a net_

B

D

F

H

_____   _____   _____   _____

Power check

How do you feel about your work in this unit?

79

Power puzzle

Cut a rectangle into 8 triangles, like this.

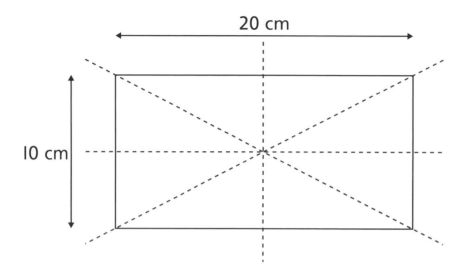

20 cm

10 cm

How many different polygons can you make using the triangles? Try using:

4 triangles   5 triangles   6 triangles   7 triangles   8 triangles

Now sort your shapes depending on features such as symmetry, or the number of obtuse angles.

The first quadrant

1 Plot the following points on the grid.

A (2,3)

B (8,1)

C (5,7)

D (0,4)

E (7,0)

F (3·5,6)

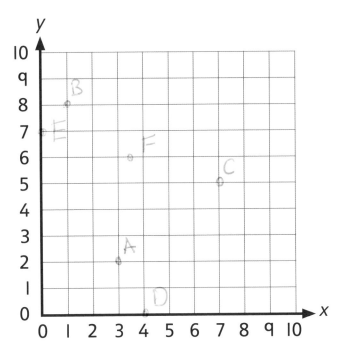

2 Write the coordinates of all the points.

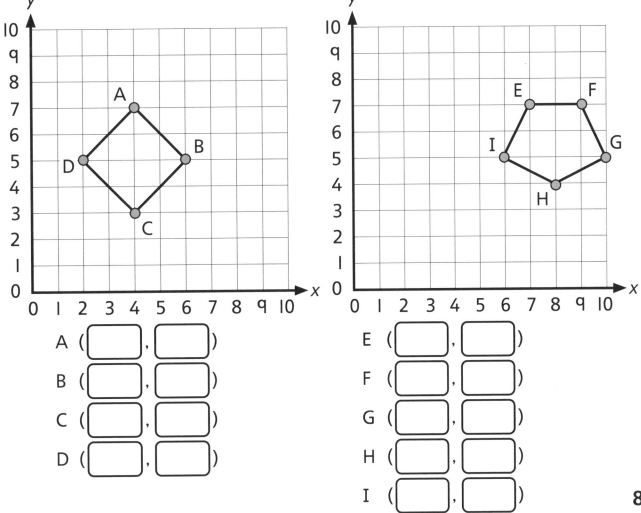

A ([   ] , [   ])

B ([   ] , [   ])

C ([   ] , [   ])

D ([   ] , [   ])

E ([   ] , [   ])

F ([   ] , [   ])

G ([   ] , [   ])

H ([   ] , [   ])

I ([   ] , [   ])

81

3 **a)** Line AB is part of a square.

What could the coordinates of the other two vertices of this square be?

(☐ , ☐)

(☐ , ☐)

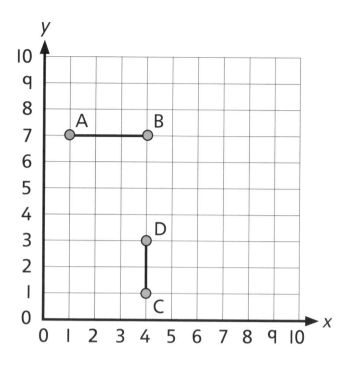

b) CD is the width of a rectangle. The length of the rectangle is twice the width. What could the coordinates of the other two vertices be?

(☐ , ☐)

(☐ , ☐)

4 The line shown is one side of a square.

a) Draw the rest of the square.

b) What are the coordinates of the vertices of the square?

(☐ , ☐)

(☐ , ☐)

(☐ , ☐)

(☐ , ☐)

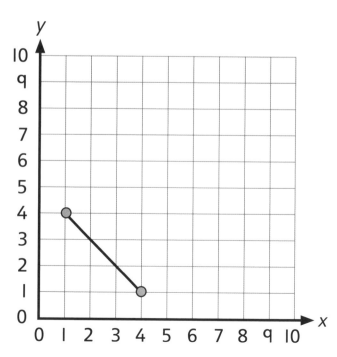

5 The sides of the three squares are all the same length.

Work out the coordinates of points A, B, C, D and E.

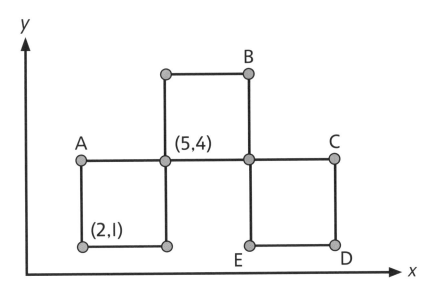

The coordinates of the points are:

A ([ ] , [ ])   D ([ ] , [ ])

B ([ ] , [ ])   E ([ ] , [ ])

C ([ ] , [ ])

Reflect

If one of the coordinates of a point is 0, what does this tell you about the point?

_____

_____

_____

83

Date: _____

Read and plot points in four quadrants

I

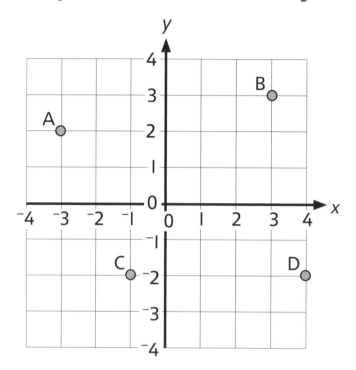

a) What are the coordinates of the points on the grid?

A (⬚ , ⬚)   C (⬚ , ⬚)

B (⬚ , ⬚)   D (⬚ , ⬚)

b) Now plot these coordinates on the grid.

E ($^-$3,$^-$2)

F (2,$^-$1)

G ($^-$1,3)

H ($^-$3,0)

I know that the first number counts along the x-axis and that the second number counts up or down the y-axis.

2 The sets of coordinates below make shapes.

Shape A coordinates: (0,2), (3,2), (⁻1,⁻2), (4,⁻2)

Shape B coordinates: (⁻5,1), (⁻3,1), (⁻2,⁻1), (⁻3,⁻2), (⁻5,⁻2), (⁻6,⁻1)

Plot the coordinates on the grid and connect them to work out the shapes.

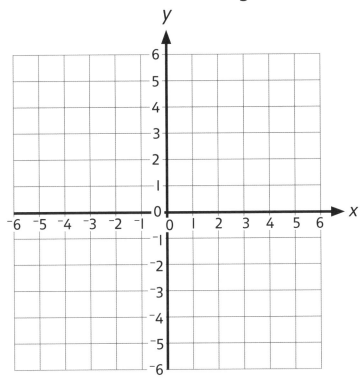

Shape A is a _____ .

Shape B is a _____ .

3 Lucy says, 'It doesn't matter which way round you write coordinates in brackets. You will always get the same point when you plot them.' Is Lucy correct? Why?

_____

_____

_____

_____

4 Mia has plotted three points of a rectangle (⁻3,3), (4,3), (4,⁻1).

What point does Mia need to plot to complete her rectangle?

CHALLENGE

> I will use the grid to plot the coordinates I know.

Mia needs to plot the point (☐ , ☐) to complete her rectangle.

Reflect

Lily says, 'It is harder to plot coordinates in all four quadrants than to plot them in just one.' Do you agree with her? Why?

_____

_____

_____

Date:_____

Translations

↓ Textbook 6C p116

1   Translate this shape 4 units right and 3 units up. Label your new shape B.

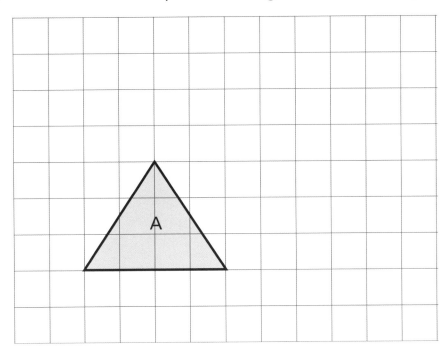

2   Translate this shape 5 units left and 1 unit down. Label your new shape D.

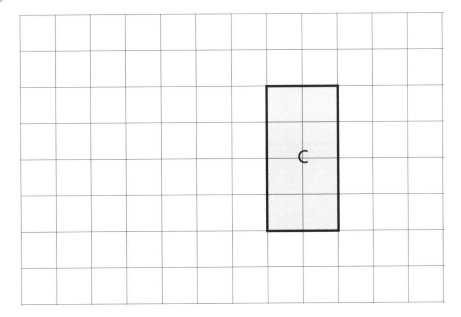

3

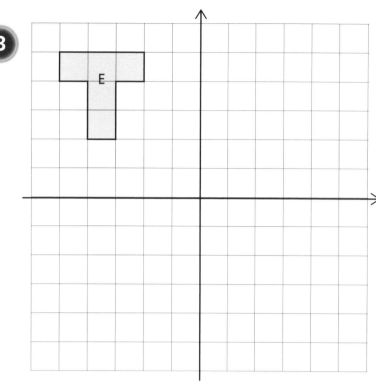

a) Translate shape E 5 units right and 4 units down. Label your new shape F.

b) Translate shape F 3 units left. Label your new shape R.

4 Complete these translations. Draw your answers on the coordinate grid.

a) Translate the rectangle 3 units right and 4 units down.

b) Translate the irregular hexagon 6 units left and 5 units up.

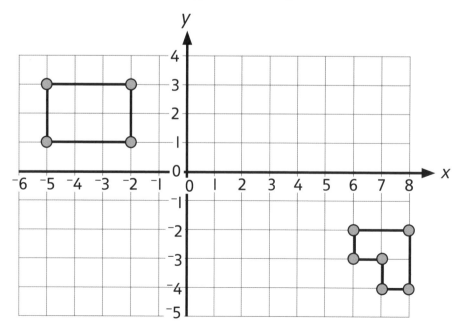

88

5 Complete these sentences.

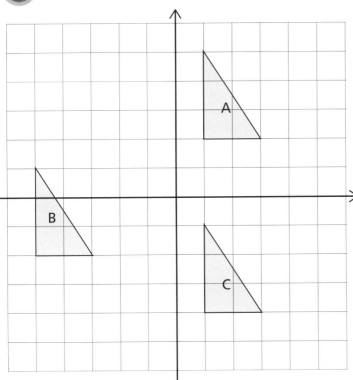

a) Shape A has been translated

☐ units left and

☐ units down onto shape B.

b) Shape A has been translated

☐ _____ onto shape C.

Reflect

Draw a shape and then translate it.

Ask a partner to describe the translation.

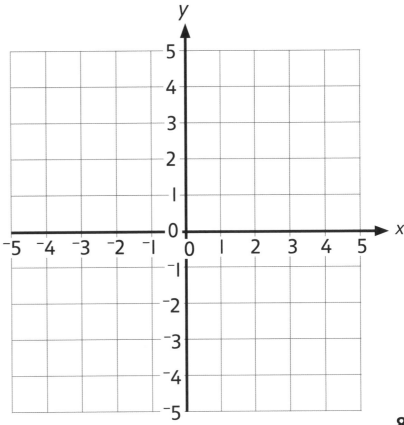

89

Date:_____

Reflections

1 **a)** Reflect this shape in the line shown. Label the shape B.

b) Reflect this shape in the line shown. Label the shape D.

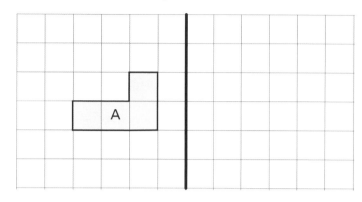

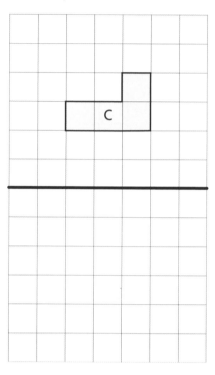

2 **a)** Reflect the triangle in the x-axis. Label the triangle B.

b) Reflect the triangle in the y-axis. Label the triangle C.

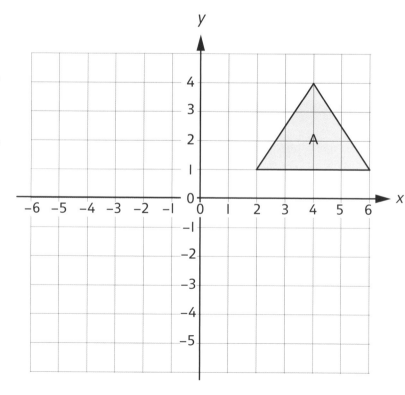

3 Complete these reflections. Draw your answers on the coordinate grid.

a) Reflect shape A in the x-axis.

b) Reflect shape B in the x-axis.

c) Reflect shape C in the y-axis.

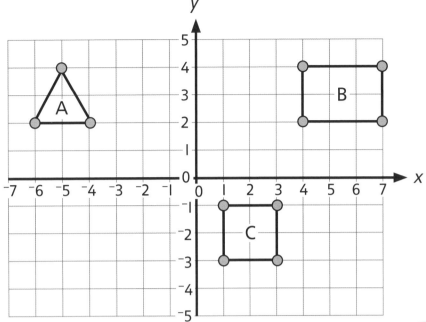

4 Reflect this shape in the diagonal line. Draw your answer on the grid.

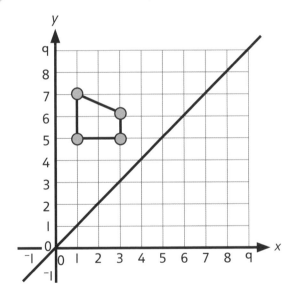

5 This rectangle is reflected in the y-axis.

Write the coordinates of the vertices of the reflected rectangle.

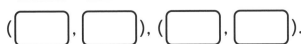

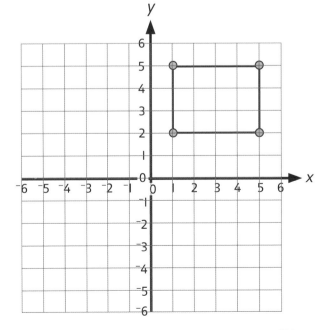

6 **a)** Reflect the shape in the left-hand grid below in the y-axis. Then translate it 1 to the right and 2 down.

b) Now translate the shape in the right-hand grid below 1 to the right and 2 down and then reflect it in the y-axis.

CHALLENGE

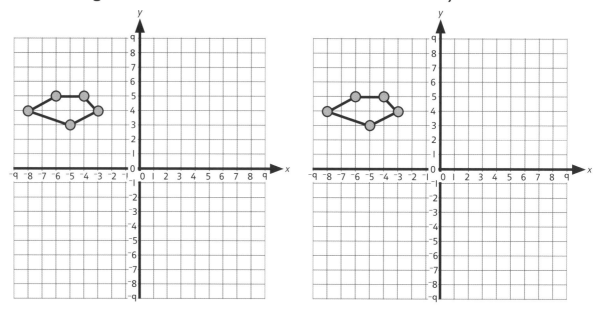

Do you get the same answer for a) and b)? Why or why not?

I do / do not get the same answers because_____

_____.

Reflect

Charlie says, 'When you reflect or translate a shape, the reflected or translated shape is identical to the shape you started with.' Is Charlie correct?

Discuss with a partner and write your answer here.

Solve problems with coordinates

1 Two vertices of a square are at the coordinates (⁻2,1) and (⁻2,⁻1).

What are the coordinates of the other two vertices of the square?

One set of possible coordinates for the other vertices are:

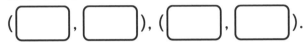

Another set of possible coordinates for the other vertices are:

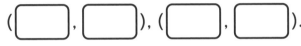

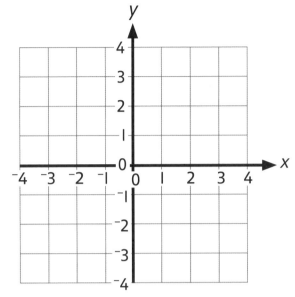

2 Squares P and Q are shown.

Square P was translated 4 units left and 8 units down to make square Q.

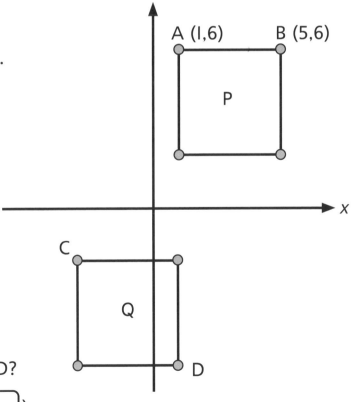

What are the coordinates of C and D?

C (⬚,⬚) D (⬚,⬚)

3 Here are two identical isosceles triangles. AC = BC and DF = EF.

a) What are the coordinates of points B and C?

The coordinates are:

B (⬚ , ⬚)

C (⬚ , ⬚)

b) What are the coordinates of points D and E?

The coordinates are:

D (⬚ , ⬚)

E (⬚ , ⬚)

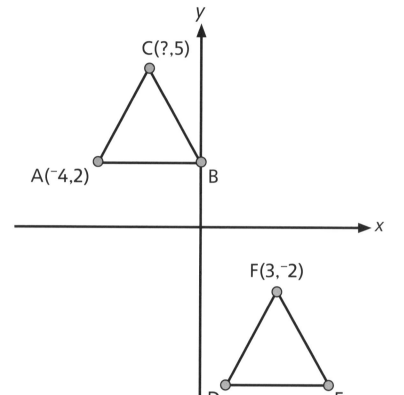

4 The length of the large square is twice the length of the small square.

Work out the coordinates of A and B.

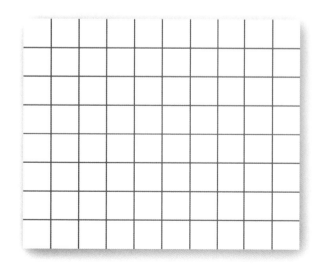

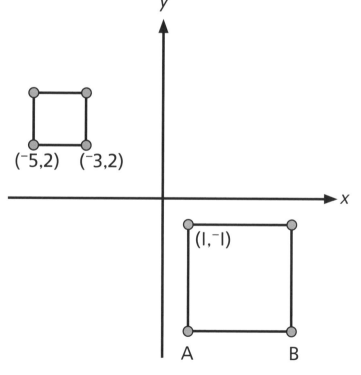

5 Below are three identical parallelograms.

Work out the coordinates of points A, B, C and D.

The coordinates of the labelled points are:

A (⬚ , ⬚)   C (⬚ , ⬚)

B (⬚ , ⬚)   D (⬚ , ⬚)

CHALLENGE

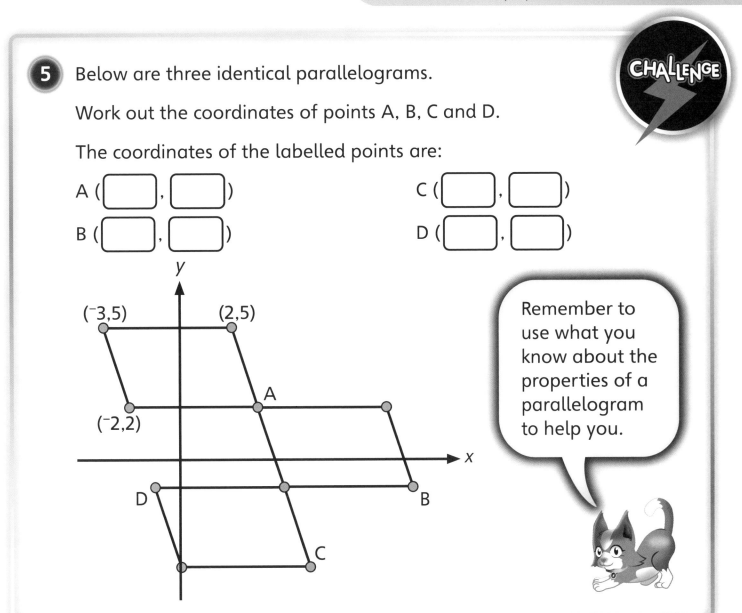

Remember to use what you know about the properties of a parallelogram to help you.

Reflect

Which problem did you find the most challenging in this lesson? Why did you find it challenging? How did you solve it?

_____

_____

_____

Date:_____

End of unit check

My journal

1 The shape on this coordinate grid is a square.

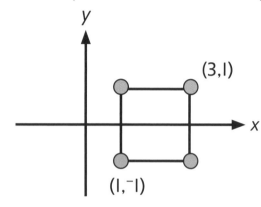

Kate says, 'It is not possible to reflect this shape in the y-axis with the information we have in the diagram.'

Is Kate correct?

Yes / No

Explain how you know.

_____

_____

_____

_____

_____

_____

2 The point on the grid below is a vertex of a rectangle.

The rectangle has side lengths of 5 units and 3 units.

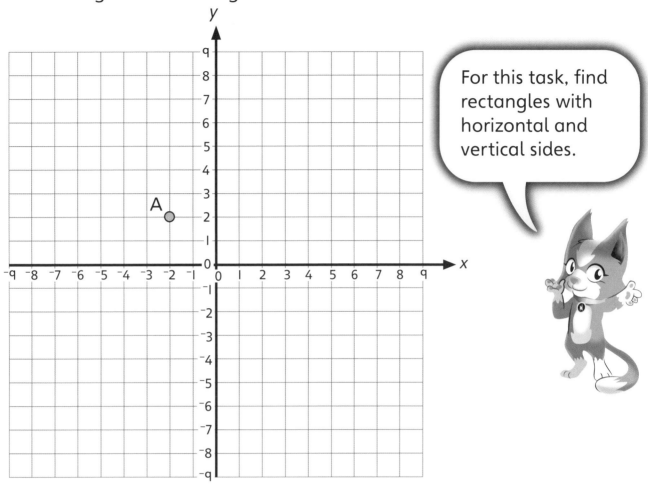

For this task, find rectangles with horizontal and vertical sides.

Draw all the possible rectangles on the grid.

Write all the possible coordinates of the other vertices of this rectangle.

_____

_____

_____

Power check

How do you feel about your work in this unit?

Power play

How can you use the properties of squares to help you find the other vertices of your partner's squares? Is it easier or harder if your partner's squares overlap? Why?

Square battleships

You need a partner to play this game.

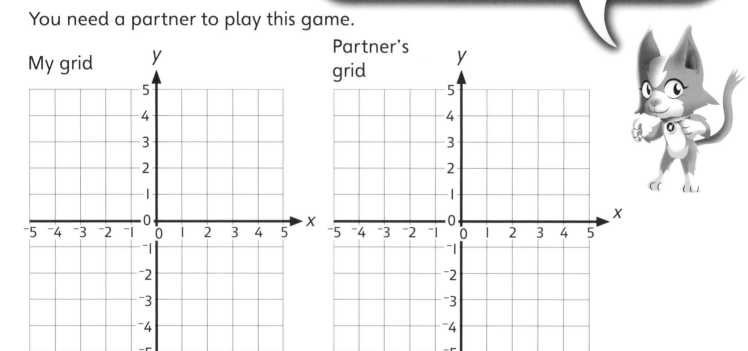

My grid

Partner's grid

How to play

1 Draw three squares on 'My grid'. Your partner should draw three squares on 'My grid' in their own book.

2 Take it in turns to guess the coordinates of the vertices of each other's squares.

Each time you guess, your partner should tell you if you have 'hit' (you have guessed a vertex correctly) or 'missed' (you have not guessed a vertex correctly).

If you have a 'hit', you should mark this vertex on the 'Partner's grid' in your book.

If you have a 'hit', you get another go.

3 The game ends when one player has found all the vertices of the other player's squares.

Date: _____

Problem solving – place value

1 The table shows children's scores for a computer game.

Put the children's scores in order starting with the smallest.

Emma, Richard, Max, Jamilla

Max	57,483
Emma	56,832
Jamilla	57,843
Richard	56,809

2 Write a number in each section of the sorting circle diagram.

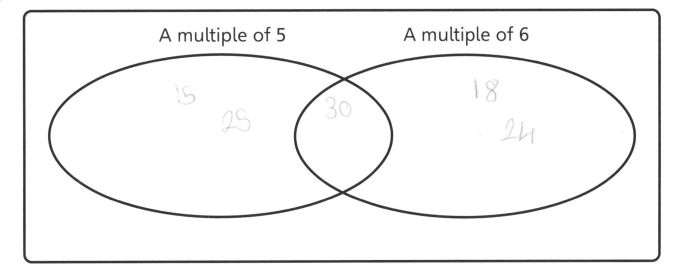

A multiple of 5   A multiple of 6

15
25
30
18
24

3 Aki has some digit cards. He uses the cards to make a 4-digit odd number that is greater than 6,800 but less than 9,000.

| 3 | 6 | 7 | 9 |

What could Aki's number be? Find all the possible answers.

6	9	7	3	7	3	6	9				
7	3	6	9								
7	6	9	3								
7	9	3	6								
7	3	9	7								
7	6	3	9								

4 The line graph shows the money made each day by a toy shop over the course of a week. The numbers on the scale are missing.

Use the graph to complete the table. Label the scale to help you.

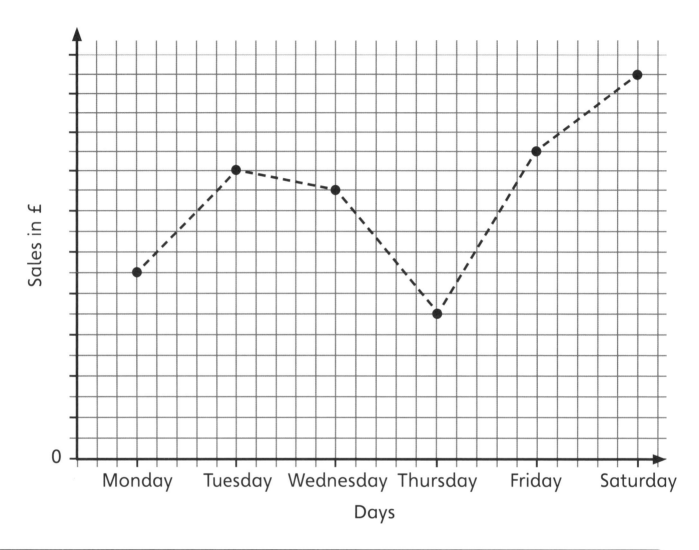

Days	Monday	Tuesday	Wednesday	Thursday	Friday	Saturday
Sales in £	1,800					

The scale is just like a number line.
I wonder what each interval represents.

CHALLENGE

5 The population of City X rounds to 483,000 to the nearest 1,000.

The population of City Y rounds to 480,000 to the nearest 10,000.

Jamie says, 'The population of City X must be larger, because 483,000 is larger than 480,000.'

Do you agree? Explain your answer.

I'm going to think about rules for rounding to help me.

_____

_____

_____

_____

Reflect

Write one more number in each section of the sorting circles.

Explain the position of 123,412 in the sorting circles.

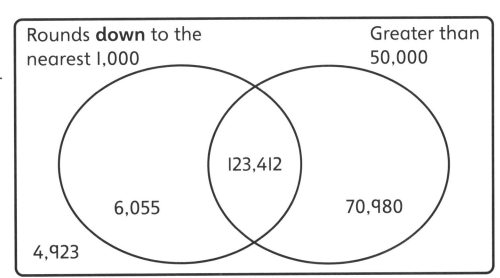

Rounds **down** to the nearest 1,000

Greater than 50,000

123,412

6,055

70,980

4,923

○ _____

○ _____

○ _____

Date: _____

Problem solving – negative numbers

1 Tick the pair of numbers that has the biggest difference.

a) ⁻4 and 12

b) ⁻8 and 9

c) ⁻20 and ⁻11

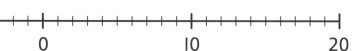

Number line from ⁻20 to 20.

2 a) This sequence increases by 7 each time.

What are the missing numbers?

☐ , ⁻16, ☐ , ⁻2, ☐ , ☐

b) This sequence decreases by the same amount each time.

What are the missing numbers?

19, 13, 7, ☐ , ⁻5, ☐

c) What is the 10th number in the sequence in part **b)**? ☐

3 This graph shows the temperature in six cities on one day in January.

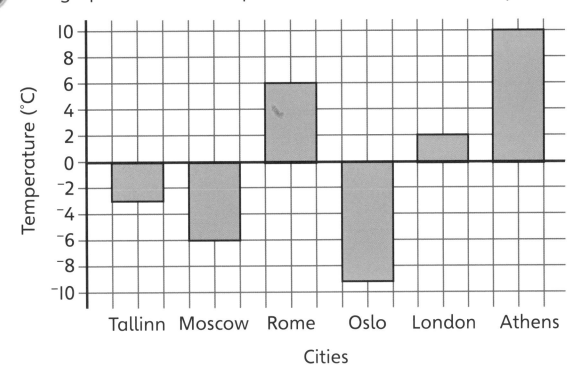

a) What is the temperature in Oslo? ☐ °C

b) Which two cities have a difference in temperature of 11 °C?

_____

4 The number line shows a winter temperature and a summer temperature in Alaska.

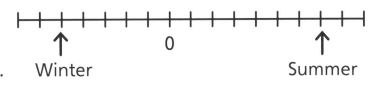

The difference between the temperatures is 48 °C.

What are the temperatures?

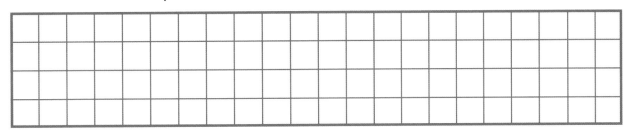

Winter temperature = ☐ °C   Summer temperature = ☐ °C

5 Work out the missing numbers on this number line.

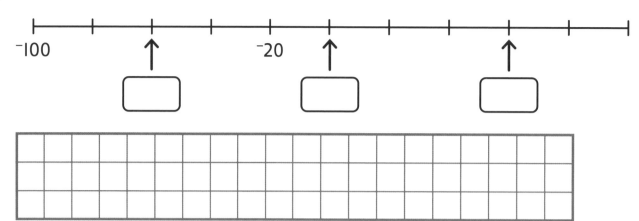

6 Arrange the numbers in the diagram so that the difference between pairs joined by a horizontal line —— is 16 and the difference between pairs joined by a dotted vertical line ┊ is 9.

CHALLENGE

⁻20   5   ⁻13

⁻4   3   ⁻11

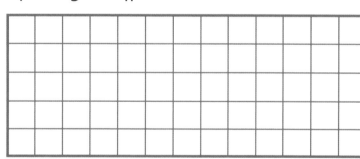

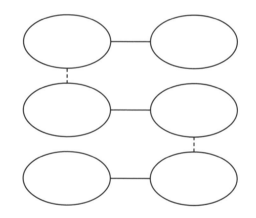

Reflect

Explain how to work out the half-way point between 24 and ⁻40.

Problem solving – addition and subtraction

1 On Tuesday morning, the number of visitors at an adventure park is 2,365. In the afternoon, 1,790 more visitors arrive but 945 go home.

How many visitors are in the park now?

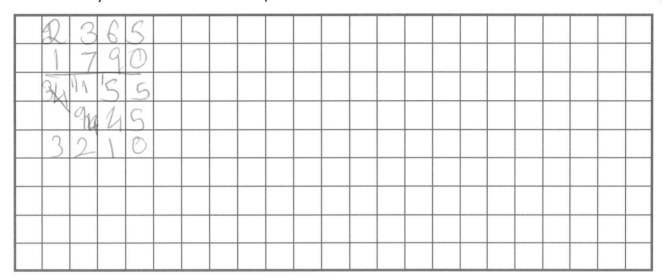

2 Andy adds three numbers together. The total is 20,000.

The first number is 4,588. The second number is 12,375.

What is the third number?

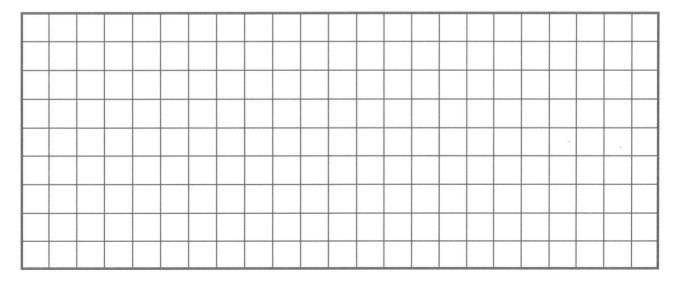

3 The bar chart shows the number of visitors at the adventure park over a weekend.

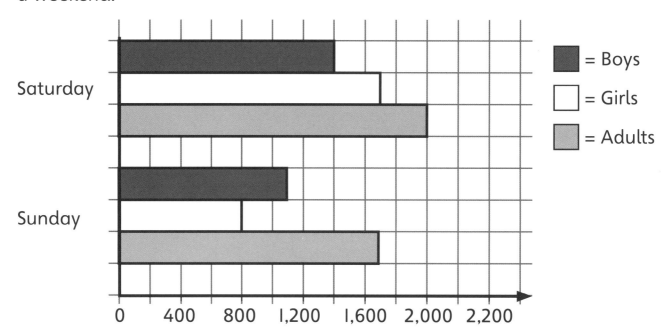

How many more children than adults visited the park on Saturday?

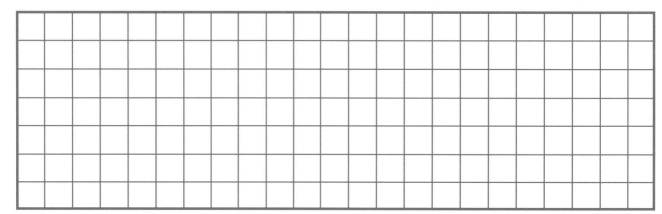

4 The Brown family sell cupcakes at a local fair. In the morning they sell 117 cupcakes.

In the afternoon they sell 48 fewer cupcakes.

How many cupcakes do they sell in total?

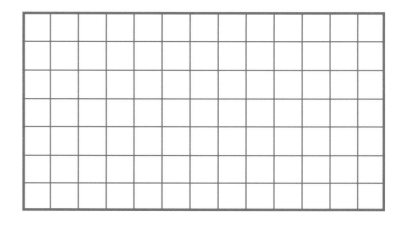

5 Write the missing digits to make these calculations correct.

a)

	Th	H	T	O	•Tth	Hth
		5	3	•	q	
+		7		8	•2	3
	1	3	2	0	•	8

b)

	Th	H	T	O
	q		7	
−	6	1		3
		q	1	8

6 Find the value of each shape.

CHALLENGE

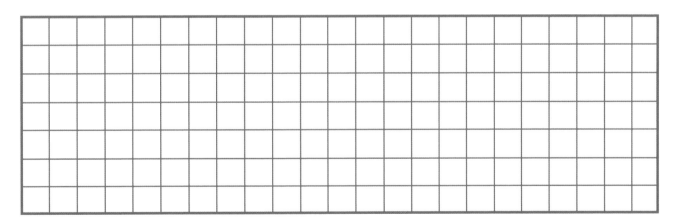

$1{,}250 - \triangle + \triangle = \pentagon$

$1{,}000 + \triangle = 1{,}600 - \square$

$700 = \square + \square$

$\triangle = \boxed{}$ $\square = \boxed{}$ $\pentagon = \boxed{}$

Reflect

Tell a partner which question you found most difficult. Explain why.

Date: _____

Problem solving – four operations ❶

1 Entry to a castle costs £6·50 more for adults than for children.

The cost for a family with one adult and four children is £49.

What is the cost of each ticket?

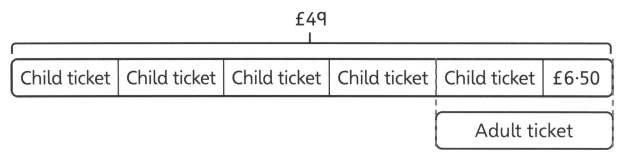

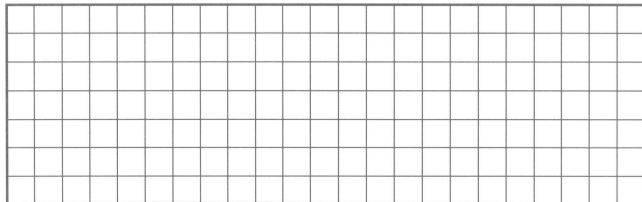

2 A supermarket needs to deliver 270 online shopping orders.

A van can carry 25 orders at a time.

How many van trips are needed to deliver all the orders?

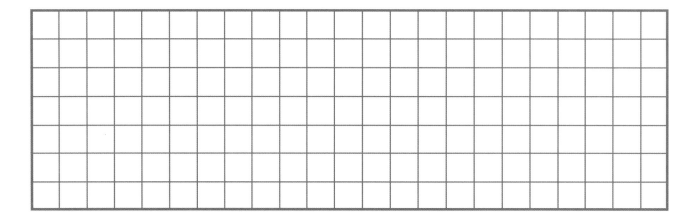

3 A supermarket sells mixed bags of 6 lemons and 4 limes.

There are 255 lemons and 171 limes to be put into bags.

a) How many mixed bags of lemons and limes can be made?

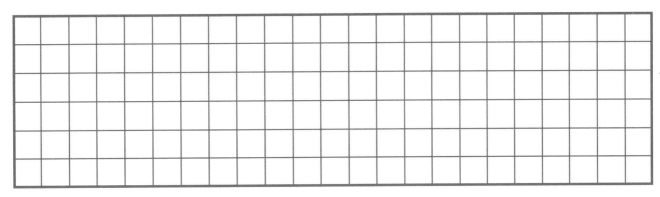

b) How many more lemons and limes are needed to complete another bag?

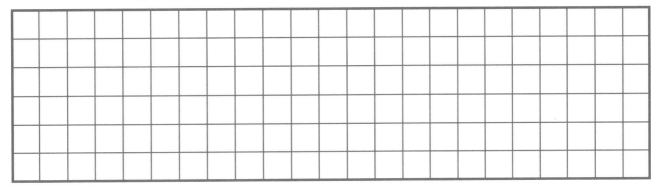

4 Cups hold 0·25 l of water. Mugs hold 375 ml of water.

Jen fills 5 cups and 5 mugs with water.

How much water does Jen use in total?

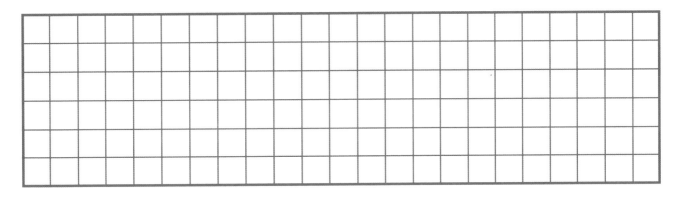

5 A number is multiplied by 6 and then divided by 3.

20 is added to the result.

Reena says, 'That is the same as doubling the number and adding 20.'

Explain why Reena is correct. Use examples to help you.

_____

_____

_____

6 There are 40 tins of blue paint. There are also tins of red paint.

The total number of litres of red paint is half the total number of litres of blue paint. How many tins of red paint are there?

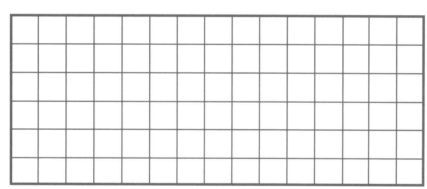

Blue

3 litres

Red

5 litres

Reflect

Write down three things you should do when solving problems.

- _____
- _____
- _____

Problem solving – four operations ❷

→ Textbook 6C p148

1 Jamie makes bracelets using a lace, 2 plain beads and 3 spotty beads.

A lace costs 25p.

This bracelet costs £1·30 to make.

The plain beads cost 18p each.

What is the cost of one spotty bead?

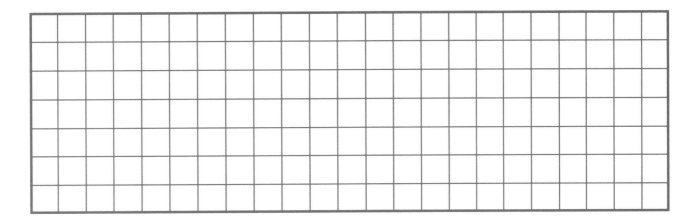

2 A tower is made with two different-sized blocks.

Calculate the height of the tower.

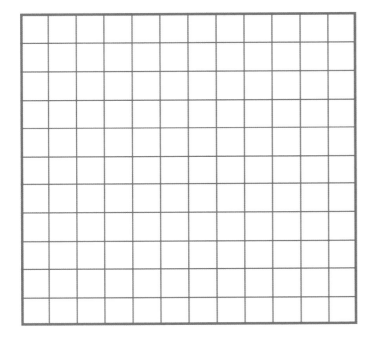

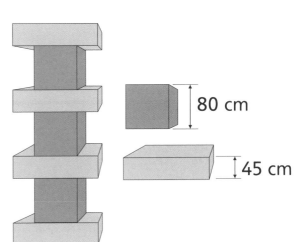

80 cm

45 cm

III

3 Richard compares the capacity of large and small bottles.

The capacity of a large bottle is 720 ml.

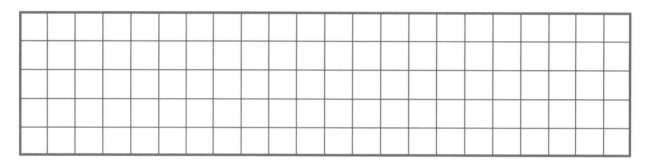

a) What is the capacity of a small bottle?

b) How many more litres of water fill 10 large bottles than fill 10 small bottles?

4 Alex uses these four digits to make a calculation:

| 3 | 4 | 8 | 9 |

Her answer is an odd multiple of 5.
She uses each number once.

What calculation did she make?
Find more than one solution and write them in the boxes.

$$\boxed{\ }\boxed{\ } \times \boxed{\ } + \boxed{\ } = \boxed{\ }$$

$$\boxed{\ }\boxed{\ } \times \boxed{\ } + \boxed{\ } = \boxed{\ }$$

$$\boxed{\ }\boxed{\ } \times \boxed{\ } + \boxed{\ } = \boxed{\ }$$

5 Find the diameters of the different-sized circles.

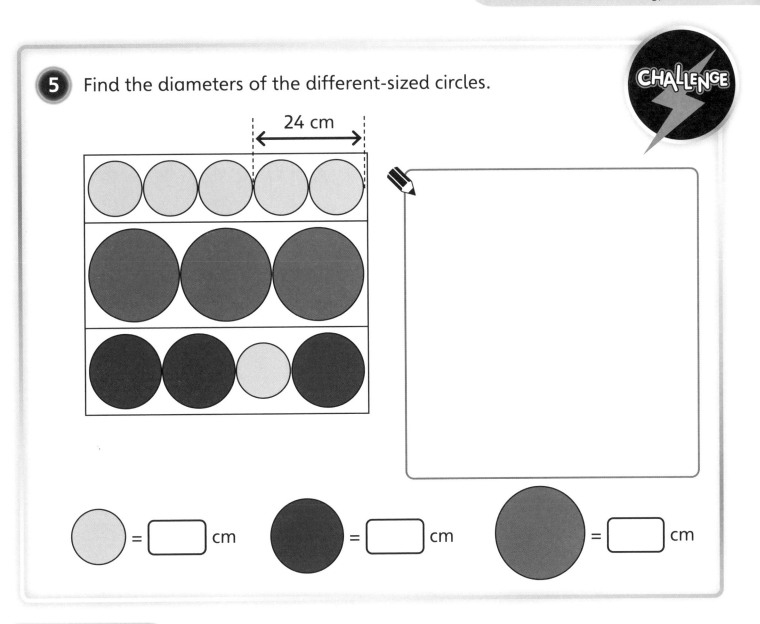

24 cm

CHALLENGE

⬜ = ⬜ cm   ⬛ = ⬜ cm   ⬤ = ⬜ cm

Reflect

Compare the strategy you used to solve question **3 b)** with a partner's strategy.

Try your strategies to find out how many more litres of water fill 25 large bottles than fill 25 small bottles.

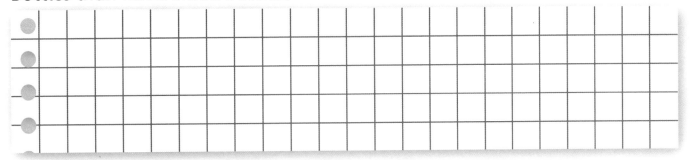

Date: _____

Problem solving – fractions

1 Use all the digit cards to make fractions that complete the statement.

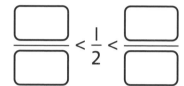 $< \frac{1}{2} <$

2 Ebo and Jamilla made 108 cookies to sell for charity.

Ebo sold $\frac{4}{9}$ of the cookies. Jamilla sold $\frac{1}{3}$ of the cookies.

a) How many cookies did they sell altogether?

b) What fraction of the cookies were left?

3 What fraction of the rectangle is **not** shaded?

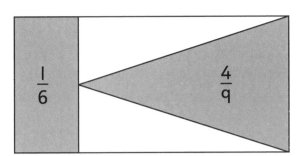

4 The distance between A and B is $1\frac{1}{4}$ km.

The distance between A and C is $4\frac{3}{5}$ km.

What is the distance from B to C?

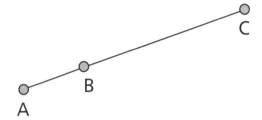

5 In a bag of marbles, 38 are green and 22 are red.

The remaining $\frac{3}{8}$ of the marbles are yellow.

How many marbles are in the bag altogether?

6 Use both of the digits 3 and 4 to make the largest possible answer to each calculation.

$$\frac{\boxed{}}{8} \times \frac{2}{\boxed{}} = \frac{\boxed{}}{\boxed{}}$$

$$\frac{\boxed{}}{5} + \frac{\boxed{}}{4} = \boxed{}\,\frac{\boxed{}}{\boxed{}}$$

$$\frac{\boxed{}}{10} + \boxed{} = \boxed{}\,\frac{\boxed{}}{\boxed{}}$$

I think I need to work out the answer each time.

I think I can use my reasoning skills to make decisions.

Reflect

$$\frac{3}{8} \quad \frac{6}{14} \quad \frac{7}{12} \quad \frac{4}{9}$$

Which of these fractions are larger than $\frac{1}{2}$? Use reasoning to explain your answer.

_____

_____

_____

Problem solving – decimals

→ Textbook 6C p156

1 The mass of a bag of sweets is 0·3 kg.

What is the mass of 5 bags of sweets?

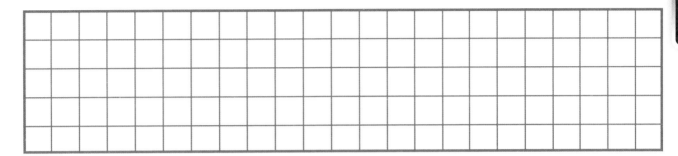

2 **a)** 4 bags of popcorn cost £7·20.

2 bags of popcorn and a carton of juice cost £4·25.

How much does the carton of juice cost?

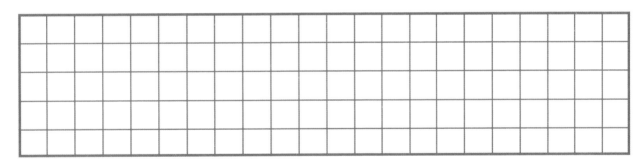

b) How much more does it cost to buy 8 bags of popcorn than 8 cartons of juice?

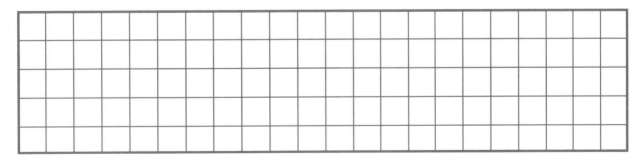

3 Write the missing numbers on the number line.

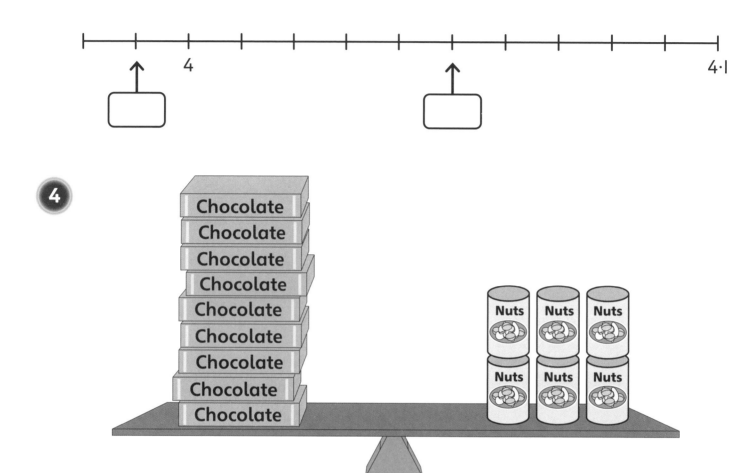

4   4·1

4

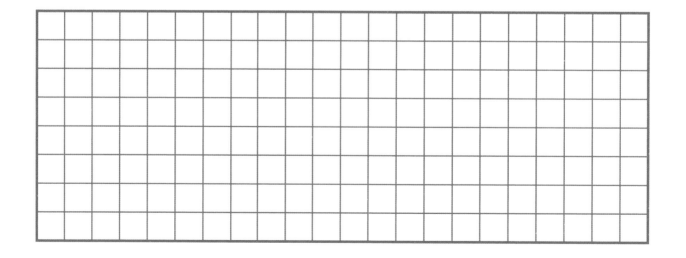

The mass of I bar of chocolate is 0·2 kg.

What is the mass of I tin of nuts?

5 Arrange the numbers in the grid so that each row, column and diagonal has the same total.

7·1   4·8   5·3

4·6   5·7   6·4   5·5

6·2   3·9

I am going to think about different totals. Not all the large numbers can go in a single row or column.

Reflect

Which of these numbers is closest to 0·9? Explain your answer.

1·2   0·87   0·08   0·95   1·01

Date: _____

Problem solving – percentages

1 A shop offers a 10% discount on sale items.

A washing machine is usually £280.

How much is the washing machine in the sale?

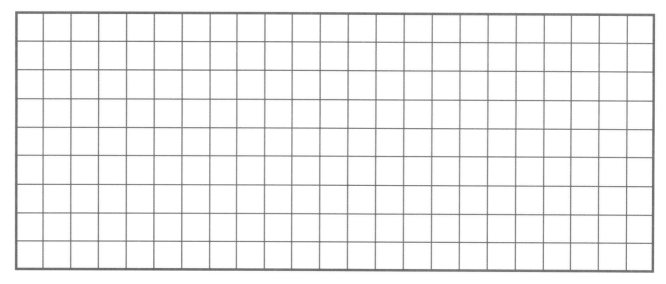

2 There are 120 children in Year 6.

30% of the children cycle to school.

25% of the children come to school by car.

The rest of the children walk to school.

How many children walk to school?

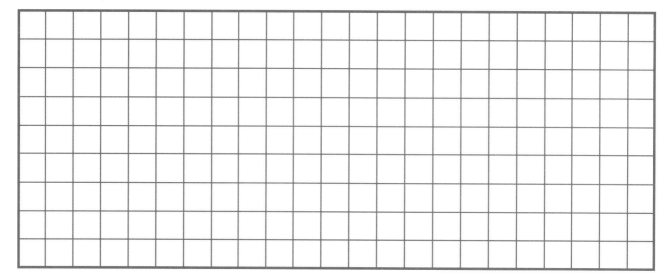

3 The table shows information about 240 daily flights from a French airport.

Complete the table.

Destination	Number of flights	Percentage of total flights
Other French cities		30%
European cities	132	
Cities outside Europe		

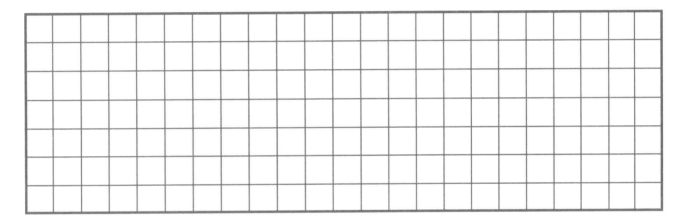

4 1,800 children visited a museum at the weekend. This number was 40% of the total number of visitors.

How many visitors were there altogether?

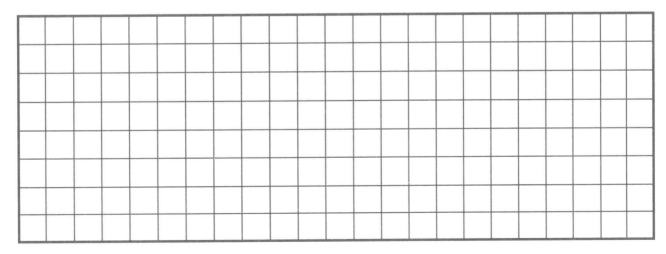

5 Complete the statement.

35% of 180 = 30% of ⬚

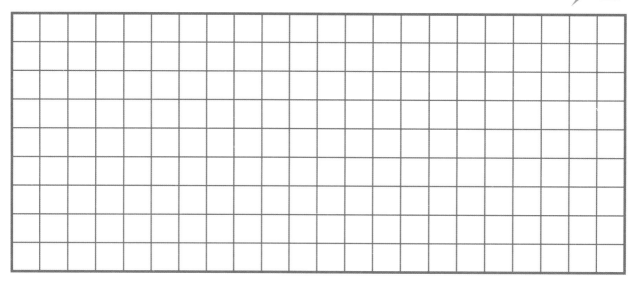

Reflect

Explain how you know that the shaded part of each shape represents 60% of its area.

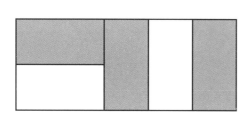
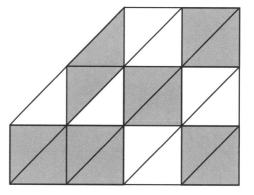

_____

_____

_____

Problem solving – ratio and proportion

1 There are 5 pencils and 3 pens in a box.

a) What fraction of the box is pens?

$\dfrac{\boxed{}}{\boxed{}}$ of the box is pens.

b) Mr Jones buys 9 of these boxes for his class.

How many fewer pens will he have than pencils?

2 A recipe uses 250 g of flour and 75 g of sugar to make 6 cakes.

a) How many cakes can be made using 375 g of sugar?

b) How much flour is needed to make 15 cakes?

123

3 Here are two rectangles.

Write the ratio of side a to side b.

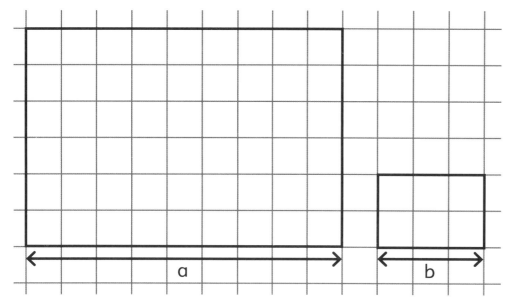

a : b = ☐ : ☐

4 On a map, I cm represents 50 km.

The distance between two cities is 650 km.

$\vdash$───$\vdash$───$\vdash$───$\vdash$───$\dashv$
0   50   100   150   200

On the map, what is the distance between the two cities?

5 $\frac{3}{8}$ of the children in a tennis club are boys.

What is the ratio of boys to girls?

124

6   8 small tins have the same mass as 5 large tins.

The mass of a small tin is 350 g.

What is the mass of a large tin?

CHALLENGE

I've seen problems like this before!

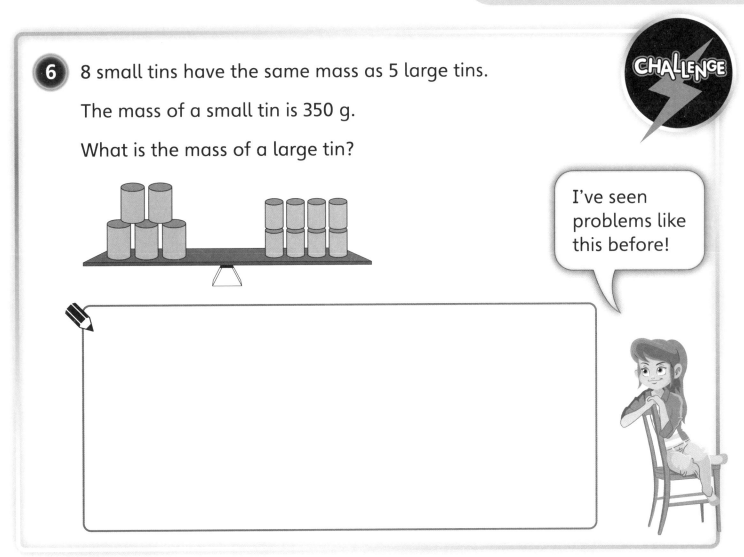

Reflect

For every 3 strawberry sweets there are 5 lime sweets in a bag.

Explain the steps needed to work out the number of lime sweets if there are 24 strawberry sweets.

_____

_____

_____

_____

125

Date: _____

Problem solving – time ❶

1 The timeline shows television programmes on 23 June.

| Live sport | Wildlife show | News | Comedy show | Comedy show |

18:45   19:25   20:25   20:45   21:45

a) Aki arrives home at 4:20 pm. How long must he wait for the start of the live sport?

b) The two comedy shows are the same length.

   Jen watches the news and one comedy show. How long does Jen watch TV for?

c) The next episode of the wildlife show is not until 2 September.

   How many **full** weeks must viewers wait?

126

Textbook 6C p168

2 A teacher makes appointments to meet with parents. Each appointment is 20 minutes long. There is a quarter of an hour break each evening.

On Tuesday, appointments start at 15:50 and end at 19:45.

On Wednesday, there are 10 appointments starting at 16:20.

a) How many appointments does the teacher make in total?

b) What time does the last appointment end on Wednesday?

3 Olivia takes part in a fun walk for charity.

She raises £8 for every full hour that she walks. She walks from 10:30 am until 4:15 pm.

How much money does she raise?

4 Which is longer, 12 intervals of 45 minutes or one-third of a day?

Explain your answer.

_____

_____

5 a) A puppy has lived for 2,904 hours. How many days is this?

CHALLENGE

b) Today is 16 October. On what date was the puppy born?

Reflect

The time is 25 minutes to 7 in the evening. Explain how to write the time
3 hours 35 minutes later in three different ways.

Problem solving – time ❷

↓ Textbook 6C p172

1 Here is part of a bus timetable.

Greytown	14:12	14:42	15:12	15:42	16:12
Oak Street	14:35	↓	15:35	16:05	↓
Ticebridge	14:53	15:20	15:53	16:23	16:50
Bankside	15:20	15:47	16:20	16:50	17:17
Chilhurst	15:45	16:12	16:45	17:15	17:42

a) How many minutes shorter is the journey from Greytown to Chilhurst on the 16:12 bus than on the 15:12 bus?

b) Mo arrives at the bus stop in Oak Street at 14:39. He wants to get to Bankside as soon as possible.

Is it quicker for him to walk 38 minutes to Ticebridge or to wait for the next bus at Oak Street?

2 This timeline shows a school day.

Lessons	Break	Lessons	Lunch break	Lessons

8:45 am   10:15 am   10:35 am   12:25 pm   1:20 pm   3:30 pm

How much more time do children spend in lessons than on breaks?

3 The line graph shows a journey Mrs Dean made in her car.

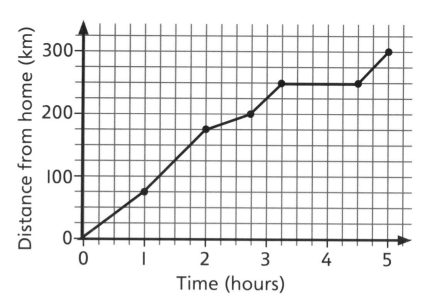

a) How far did she travel in the first 90 minutes?

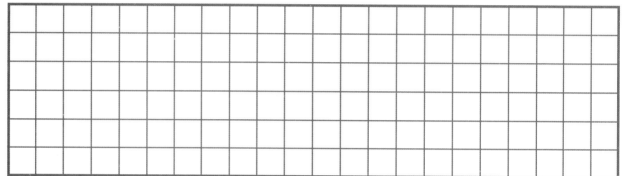

b) She stopped for a lunch break. How long was this break?

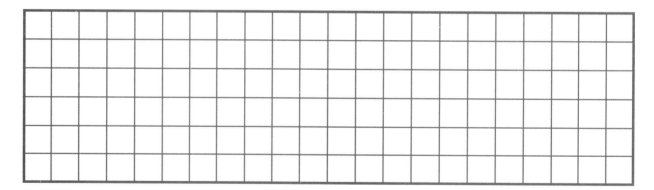

c) Mrs Dean left home at 09:50. At what time did she stop for lunch?

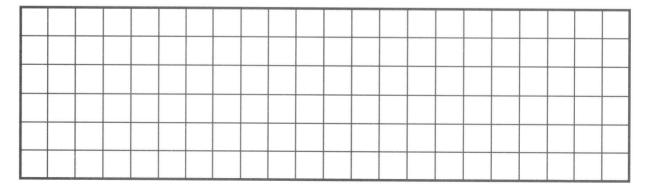

4 The table shows the costs of some taxi journeys. The taxi companies charge per minute.

 CHALLENGE

Taxi company	Departure time	Arrival time	Cost
A	10:10 am	10:35 am	£15
B	11:50 am	12:05 pm	£9·75
C	12:10 pm	12:15 pm	£3·20

Richard wants to go on a 30-minute journey. Which taxi company will be the cheapest?

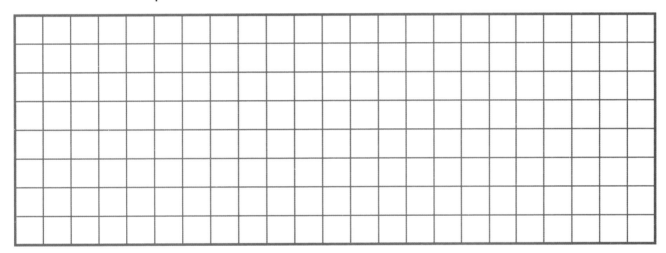

Reflect

Lexi says, 'The time is 12:45. In 1 hour 55 minutes, it will be 14:00.'

What mistake has she made? What is the correct answer?

Date: _____

Problem solving – position and direction

1 The points A, B, C and D are equally spaced along the line AD.

What are the coordinates of B and D?

B ()

D ()

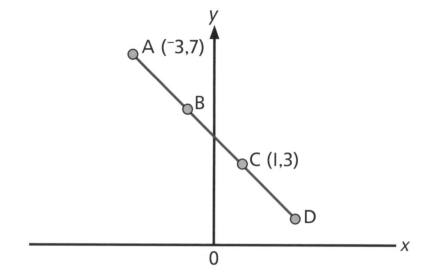

2 **a)** Reflect the rhombus in the y-axis. Use a ruler.

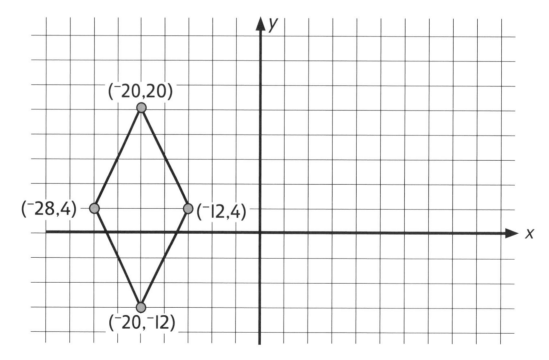

b) Write the coordinates of the vertices in the reflected shape.

 ,  ,

3 This trapezium is reflected in a mirror line.

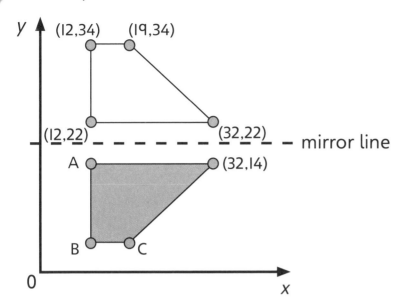

a) What are the coordinates of vertices A, B and C in the reflected shape?

A (⬚ , ⬚)   B (⬚ , ⬚)   C (⬚ , ⬚)

b) What are the coordinates of the point half-way between A and B?

(⬚ , ⬚)

c) Circle the coordinates that are inside the reflected shape.

(12,16)   (32,12)   (22,2)   (16,12)   (16,15)

4 The points A and B are two vertices of a right-angled triangle.

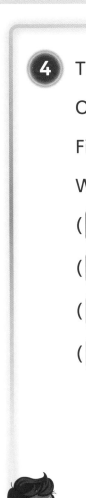

CHALLENGE

One side of the triangle has been drawn on the grid.

Find four possible positions for the third vertex, C.

Write the coordinates.

I wonder whether AB is the long side or one of the shorter sides of the triangle.

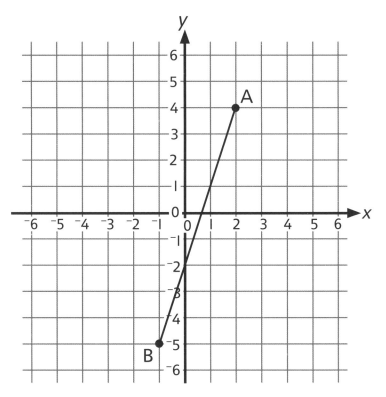

Reflect

Two coordinates (7,2) and (7,10) are plotted on a grid.
Explain how to find the coordinates of the half-way point.

Problem solving – properties of shapes

1 Calculate the angles a, b, c and d in these diagrams.

a)

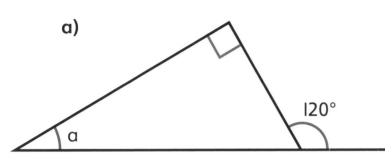

120°

a

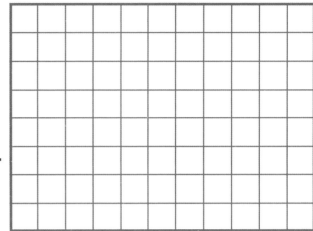

b)

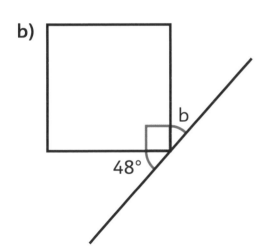

b

48°

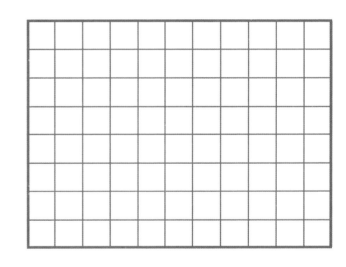

c)

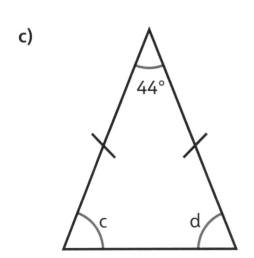

44°

c   d

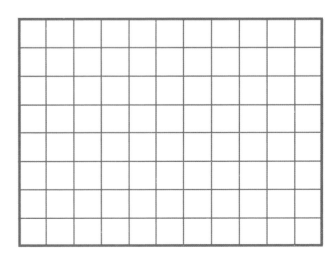

2 **a)** Calculate the sizes of angles a and b.

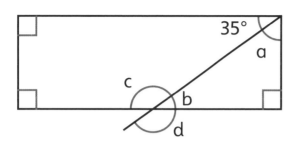 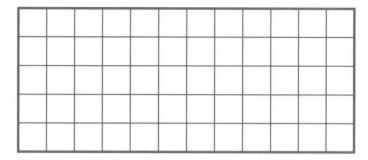

b) Explain how you can now find the sizes of angles c and d.

_____

_____

_____

3 A scalene triangle is drawn inside a square. Calculate the sizes of angles x, y and z.

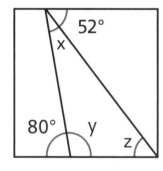 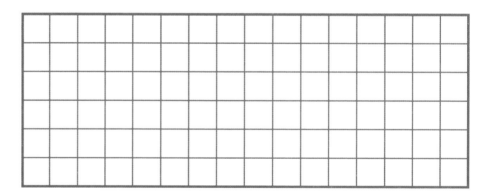

4 Three angles meet at a point. Angle x is 40° larger than angle y. Angle z is double the size of angle x. What is the size of each angle?

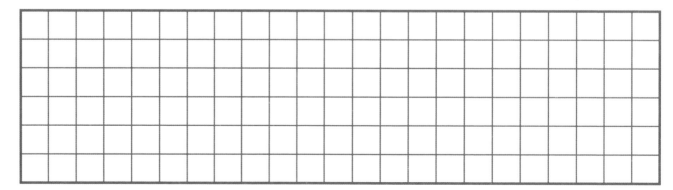

5 Calculate the sizes of angles a, b and c.

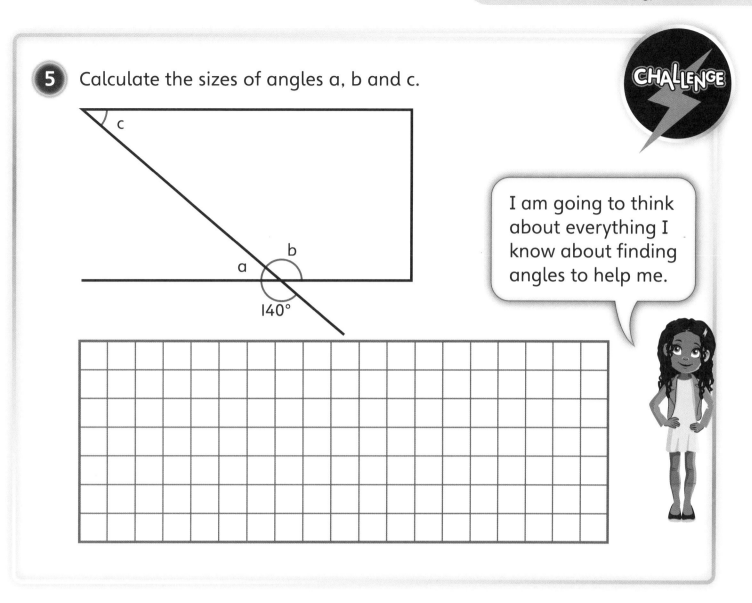

CHALLENGE

> I am going to think about everything I know about finding angles to help me.

Reflect

Three angles, a, b and c, are on a straight line. Angle a is 88°.

What could be the sizes of angles b and c? Find at least two solutions. Explain your answers.

- _____
- _____
- _____

Date: _____

Problem solving – properties of shapes ➋

1 A regular octagon is drawn on a line.

Calculate the size of angle m.

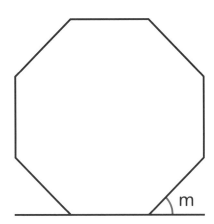

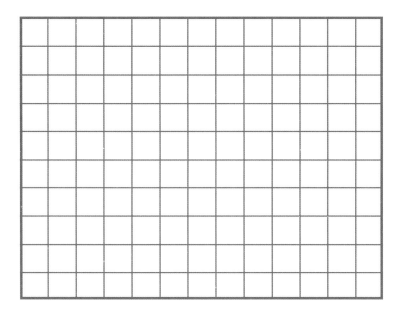

2 Circle all the shapes that are named in the wrong section of the table.

Draw an arrow to show which section they should be in.

	Interior angles add up to 360°	Interior angles do not add up to 360°
Have at least one pair of parallel sides	Rectangle Parallelogram	Rhombus Regular pentagon
Have no pairs of parallel sides	Kite Trapezium	Triangle Regular hexagon

3 Here is a pattern of regular hexagons.

What calculation can you use to prove that the interior angles of three regular hexagons meet around a point?

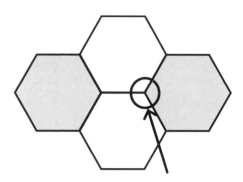

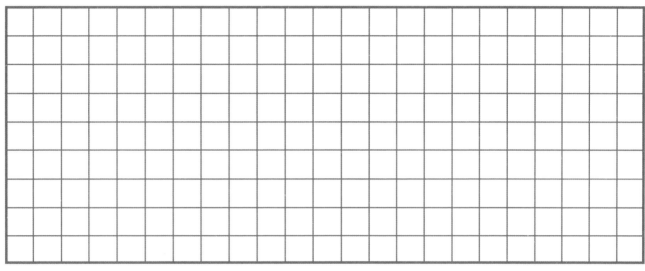

4 Calculate the sizes of angles a and b.

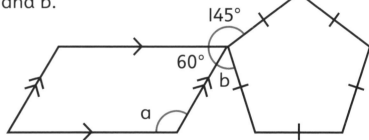

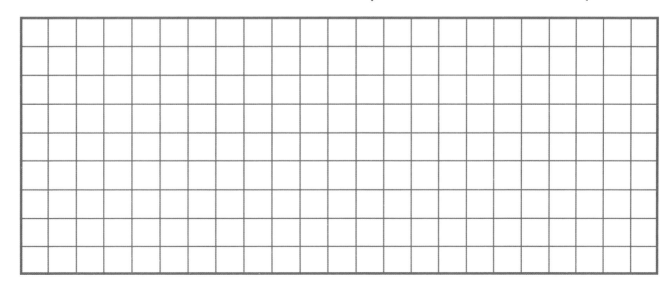

5 Aki draws an irregular hexagon.

Angles a, b, c and d add up to 600°.

Angle e is double the size of angle f.

Calculate the sizes of angles e and f.

Reflect

Three of the angles in a pentagon add up to to 330°.

Explain how you know that the pentagon is not regular.

_____

_____

_____

End of unit check

→ Textbook 6C p188

My journal

Toshi earns £1,200 a month.

He spends 25% on his rent.

He spends $\frac{3}{10}$ on food and entertainment.

He uses the rest to pay bills and to save some money too.

For every £3 he spends on bills, he saves £2.

How much will he save in 3 years?

Explain each of your steps. Did you get stuck? If so, where?

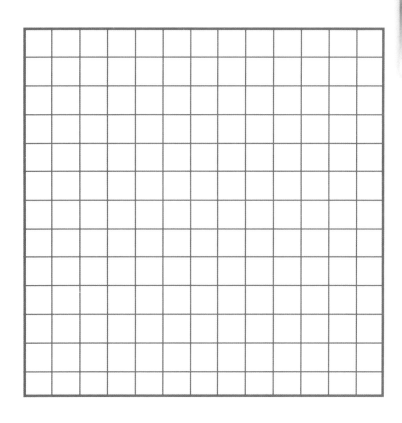

_____

_____

_____

_____

_____

Power check

How do you feel about your work in this unit?

Power puzzle

I spent three times as much money at the fair as Max, but I was there for half the time.

Jamie

I spent a quarter of the money that Zac spent at the fair. I arrived at 10:30 and left at 13:00.

Max

I spent £10 at the fair. I spent 45 minutes longer at the fair than Jamie.

Zac

Complete the table about the children's day at the fair.

	Money spent	Arrival time	Departure time
Jamie			14:15
Max			
Zac		11:15	

Write a similar problem about two or three characters. Give it to a partner to solve. Remember – you need to have worked out the answer!

Published by Pearson Education Limited, 80 Strand, London, WC2R 0RL.

www.pearsonschools.co.uk

Text © Pearson Education Limited 2018, 2023
Edited by Pearson and Florence Production Ltd
First edition edited by Pearson, Little Grey Cells Publishing Services and Haremi Ltd
Designed and typeset by Pearson, Florence Production Ltd and PDQ Digital Media Solutions Ltd
First edition designed and typeset by Kamae Design
Original illustrations © Pearson Education Limited 2018, 2023
Illustrated by Diego Diaz, Adam Linley and Nadene Naude at Beehive Illustration; and Kamae Design
Images: The Royal Mint, 1971, 1982, 1990, 1997, 1998: 37, 64
Cover design by Pearson Education Ltd
Front and back cover illustrations by Diego Diaz and Nadene Naude at Beehive Illustration

Series Editor: Tony Staneff
Lead author: Josh Lury
Consultants (first edition): Professor Liu Jian and Professor Zhang Dan

The rights of Tony Staneff and Josh Lury to be identified as authors of this work have been asserted by them in accordance with the Copyright, Designs and Patents Act 1988.

This publication is protected by copyright, and permission should be obtained from the publisher prior to any prohibited reproduction, storage in a retrieval system, or transmission in any form or by any means, electronic, mechanical, photocopying, recording, or otherwise. For information regarding permissions, request forms and the appropriate contacts, please visit https://www.pearson.com/us/contact-us/permissions.html Pearson Education Limited Rights and Permissions Department

First published 2018
This edition first published 2023

27 26 25 24 23
10 9 8 7 6 5 4 3 2 1

British Library Cataloguing in Publication Data
A catalogue record for this book is available from the British Library

ISBN 978 1 292 41966 4

Printed in the UK by Bell & Bain Ltd, Glasgow

For Power Maths resources go to
www.activelearnprimary.co.uk

Note from the publisher
Pearson has robust editorial processes, including answer and fact checks, to ensure the accuracy of the content in this publication, and every effort is made to ensure this publication is free of errors. We are, however, only human, and occasionally errors do occur. Pearson is not liable for any misunderstandings that arise as a result of errors in this publication, but it is our priority to ensure that the content is accurate. If you spot an error, please do contact us at resourcescorrections@pearson.com so we can make sure it is corrected.